Praise for *Solvable*

'Central to business is problem solving, and the types of problems businesses face are increasingly complex and ill defined. To solve problems, we increasingly need therefore to think explicitly about the problem of how to best solve the problem and to hone our problem solving skills. The authors provide an accessible and pragmatic framework for doing so, covering the whole cycle of solving problems including framing, assessing, deciding, engaging, and implementing. It will be a welcome addition to any manager's armoury.'

Martin Reeves, Chairman, BCG Henderson Institute

'*Solvable* is an evidence-based guide to making good decisions. In an uncertain world, the essence of good decision making is informed reflection. This book walks the reader through the process of reflection – thinking about how we think about decisions, what to pay attention to, and how to bring the necessary resources together in doing so. Step by step, it lays out evidence-based processes for scoping the decision (and the problem to be solved), gathering information, making the decision and acting on it. Full of examples showing the good, the bad, and the ugly in modern decision making, *Solvable* builds the decision maker's confidence and competence. I am singing its praises to my students and colleagues!'

Denise M. Rousseau, H. J. Heinz II University Professor of Organizational Behavior and Public Policy; Director, Project on Evidence-based Organizational Practices, Heinz College and Tepper School of Business, Carnegie Mellon University

'Every manager strives to make good decisions for the organisation—yet, all too often biases, false assumptions or oversimplifications hamper their ability to do just that! By drawing on scientific insights and their vast personal experience, Chevallier and Enders guide you through three main steps (frame, explore, decide) that are indispensable for solving complex problems. In short: A 'must read' for current and aspiring managers!'

Marc Gruber, Professor of Entrepreneurship & Technology Commercialization, École Polytechnique Fédérale de Lausanne

'In *Solvable* Albrecht and Arnaud provide a useful and straightforward framework for approaching complex problem solving, whether in business or more broadly in life. But the real added value for me, as is so often the case for great business books, are the real-world examples from corporations, governments and individuals around the world, struggling as they face urgent, complex challenges. Nothing makes a lesson clearer than a great example of how it wasn't applied. Recommended.'

Ian Charles Stewart, Co-Founder, *Wired Magazine*

'Strong problem-solving capabilities are essential, especially when you confront complex problems that have a profound and long-lasting impact on your organisations. *Solvable* provides a thorough-yet-accessible approach to help you elevate your complex problem-solving game.'

Jørgen Vig Knudstorp, Executive Chairman, Lego Brand Group

'*Solvable* is a brilliant book: hands-on, humorous, deeply researched, well written, and stuffed to the brim with memorable stories and real-world cases. Read this if you want to become a world-class problem solver at work and in life.'

Thomas Wedell-Wedellsborg, author of *What's Your Problem* and *Innovation as Usual*, Harvard Business Review Press

'Whether deciding on a career path or inventing a new medical technology, people are searching for, engaging in, and solving complex and ill-defined problems during most of their waking lives. With the goal of moving people toward a better problem space more often (and away from suboptimal distractions), the authors present a systematic approach to the broad problem-solving process, masterfully engaging readers with their accessible writing, clear examples, and scientific support. This book stands to have wide appeal to anyone engaging with real-world problems: innovators and investors, employees and educators, scientists and students.'

Fred Oswald, PhD, Professor and Herbert S. Autrey Chair in Social Sciences, Department of Psychological Sciences, Rice University

'The authors simplify the massive research literature on flaws in human judgement but they don't over-simplify it. The result is a superb practical guide for improving our problem-solving and decision-making skills in everyday life.'

Philip Tetlock, Annenberg University Professor, University of Pennsylvania

'*Solvable* is a valuable guide to making good decisions in situations of high complexity. Using many fascinating and entertaining examples, Chevallier and Enders offer useful guides for organising thought and triggering insight. Their metaphor of the Hero and Dragon is an artful way of describing the value of focusing on the crux of a challenge.'

Richard Rumelt, Professor Emeritus, UCLA Anderson School of Management, and author of *Good Strategy/Bad Strategy*

'The world changed, almost overnight. For good, not just for a year or two. There is nobody you can call to reverse it. That's when you need a lot more than a forecast. You need options, criteria and choices for the new world. Read the book.'

Jouko Karvinen, Chairman of the Board, Finnair

'While I believe the book can be very practical for everyday management as it provides tools and support for effective, impactful and long-lasting, problem solving, it is very useful for developing leaders with an open and transformational mindset for their organisation. From smart answers to uncovering questions starting with a why or a how, this book helps leaders with the language, the tone and the posture they take so their organisation develops the muscle of solving problems, transforming the unacceptable of today into a breakthrough of tomorrow.'

Gilles Morel, President EMEA and EVP, Whirlpool Corporation

Solvable

Pearson

At Pearson, we have a simple mission: to help people make more of their lives through learning.

We combine innovative learning technology with trusted content and educational expertise to provide engaging and effective learning experiences that serve people wherever and whenever they are learning.

From classroom to boardroom, our curriculum materials, digital learning tools and testing programmes help to educate millions of people worldwide – more than any other private enterprise.

Every day our work helps learning flourish, and wherever learning flourishes, so do people.

To learn more, please visit us at **www.pearson.com/uk**

Solvable

A simple solution to
complex problems

Arnaud Chevallier and Albrecht Enders

Pearson

Harlow, England • London • New York • Boston • San Francisco • Toronto • Sydney • Dubai • Singapore • Hong Kong
Tokyo • Seoul • Taipei • New Delhi • Cape Town • São Paulo • Mexico City • Madrid • Amsterdam • Munich • Paris • Milan

PEARSON EDUCATION LIMITED
KAO Two
KAO Park
Harlow CM17 9NA
United Kingdom
Tel: +44 (0)1279 623623
Web: www.pearson.com/uk

First edition published 2022 (print and electronic)

ISBN: 978-1-292-37428-4 (print)
          978-1-292-37427-7 (PDF)
          978—1292-37426-0 (ePub)

British Library Cataloguing-in-Publication Data
A catalogue record for the print edition is available from the British Library

Library of Congress Cataloging-in-Publication Data
A catalog record for the print edition is available from the Library of Congress

10 9 8 7 6 5 4 3 2 1
26 25 24 23 22

Cover design by Two Associates

Print edition typeset in 10/13 pt and SST by Straive

NOTE THAT ANY PAGE CROSS REFERENCES REFER TO THE PRINT EDITION

To Leslie, my biggest fan. Thank you for all your wonderful support! (Arnaud)

To Kim, Megan, Julia and Max. For gently encouraging me to reframe on a daily basis. (Albrecht)

CONTENTS

___

Pearson's Commitment to Diversity, Equity and Inclusion

Pearson is dedicated to creating bias-free content that reflects the diversity, depth and breadth of all learners' lived experiences. We embrace the many dimensions of diversity including, but not limited to, race, ethnicity, gender, sex, sexual orientation, socioeconomic status, ability, age and religious or political beliefs.

Education is a powerful force for equity and change in our world. It has the potential to deliver opportunities that improve lives and enable economic mobility. As we work with authors to create content for every product and service, we acknowledge our responsibility to demonstrate inclusivity and incorporate diverse scholarship so that everyone can achieve their potential through learning. As the world's leading learning company, we have a duty to help drive change and live up to our purpose to help more people create a better life for themselves and to create a better world.

Our ambition is to purposefully contribute to a world where:

- Everyone has an equitable and lifelong opportunity to succeed through learning.
- Our educational products and services are inclusive and represent the rich diversity of learners.
- Our educational content accurately reflects the histories and lived experiences of the learners we serve.
- Our educational content prompts deeper discussions with students and motivates them to expand their own learning and worldview.

We are also committed to providing products that are fully accessible to all learners. As per Pearson's guidelines for accessible educational Web media, we test and retest the capabilities of our products against the highest standards for every release, following the WCAG guidelines in developing new products for copyright year 2022 and beyond. You can learn more about Pearson's commitment to accessibility at:

https://www.pearson.com/us/accessibility.html

While we work hard to present unbiased, fully accessible content, we want to hear from you about any concerns or needs regarding this Pearson product so that we can investigate and address them.

- Please contact us with concerns about any potential bias at:
  https://www.pearson.com/report-bias.html

- For accessibility-related issues, such as using assistive technology with Pearson products, alternative text requests, or accessibility documentation, email the Pearson Disability Support team at:
  disability.support@pearson.com

FOREWORD

———

Making good decisions is a deliberately acquired skill. Learning this skill requires conscientious attention to some fundamentals: Decisions fall into some basic categories; the category determines the process most likely to produce a good result; and reflecting on results improves subsequent decisions. Furthering your decision skills takes deliberate practice repeated over time in a process that looks like this:

Although the decision process depends on the category of decision under consideration, there are common denominators that help with any complex decisions. *Solvable* builds on 40 years of problem-solving research in organisations to help readers manage the decisions arising in organisations.

As Arnaud Chevallier and Albrecht Enders show, the heart of making a good decision is using a good *process*. This book walks the reader through the decision steps that work best for each problem type. We know a lot about how to make a good decision when information is abundant and the problem familiar, how to make a good decision when information is limited and the problem novel, and other decision types in between. This book helps the reader understand how evidence-based decision processes work, and how to choose an appropriate process for the information you have and the uncertainty you face.

Importantly, *Solvable* addresses both the technical side and the people side of problem solving, giving concrete ways to adopt an evidence-based approach while managing the key stakeholders whose insights, ideas and support are needed for success.

In addition, since solving complex problems occurs under uncertainty, we must adopt a probabilistic mindset, updating our thinking as new evidence surfaces. The book proposes a concrete way of doing this, treating the process as an iterative one.

Since the early days of process improvement from Scientific Management to Toyota Production Systems, it has been understood that if you want to improve a process you first need to standardise it. That means you must understand what you did to produce the results you got. Reflection is key. Experience is not enough. No complex skill is acquired without the mental effort to make sense of how and why results came about. Ask yourself and your team, what assumptions were made? How did they affect what happened? Was there a difference between what was expected and what occurred? What was done that could have been done differently? With practice and feedback, you can make that process work better and better. This thoughtful practical book boils down consistent findings from scholarly research into concrete actions that improve your decision-making skills and the quality of the decisions you make.

Denise M. Rousseau

Carnegie Mellon University

Pittsburgh, PA USA

PROLOGUE

——

For decades, Boeing and Airbus shared the majority of the passenger-carrying jet market. Boeing arrived first in 1967 with the 737 and developed an early lead during the two decades it took Airbus to enter with its A320. Subsequently, both companies updated their airframe regularly, but complete overhauls were rare. By 2010, Airbus hadn't refreshed the A320's design since its 1988 launch, while Boeing's last refresh dated to 1997, when the 737's third generation, the 737NG, had made its début.

Long time the underdog, Airbus had been playing catchup. But in December 2010 it announced that it had stealthily developed a more efficient version of the A320, the A320neo, for 'new engine option'. This new design was attractive, burning 6% less fuel than Boeing's most advanced model. Airbus' order books quickly filled up, even winning over American Airlines, a Boeing-exclusive customer until then.

At that time, Boeing had been debating the future of its narrow-body jet programme for many months, oscillating between updating its workhorse 737 yet again and launching a new design. Now facing intense market pressure, Boeing's executives made their decision in a matter of weeks, announcing that they would launch a fourth-generation 737, the Max, in record time.

The implications of this decision were dramatic. The original 737 was designed at a time when many airports lacked infrastructure. Planes that were lower to the ground were attractive, with fewer steps to climb when boarding and easily accessed cargo areas. In contrast, when Airbus designed its A320, many of these constraints had vanished, enabling it to build a plane positioned higher. This difference now played a critical role as the new fuel-efficient engines were bigger than previous generations; small enough to fit on an A320 but big enough that the 737 required some structural modifications to achieve the required ground clearance.

These modifications affected handling and, in some circumstances, could lead the plane to tip skyward, risking a mid-air stall. Boeing addressed this issue with a software solution, an automated system called 'Maneuvering Characteristics Augmentation System' (MCAS). When it sensed that a stall was impending, the MCAS pushed the nose of the plane downward. With this solution in place, Boeing quickly revved up its production, and the Max made its maiden commercial flight in January 2016. Designed and produced in record time, it gave Boeing the response it needed to the A320neo. For a while, it looked like Boeing had pulled off the impossible.

However, after two fatal crashes in 2018 and 2019, the Max was grounded by regulators worldwide. Investigations soon revealed that MCAS activated automatically, without pilot intervention. They also revealed that, in an effort to keep training costs low and avoid the need for pilots to re-certify when transitioning to the Max, Boeing had chosen not to inform pilots about the MCAS nor explain how to disengage it. The MCAS was soon implicated in the crashes, and fatal design flaws surfaced.

By not deciding between revamping their existing airframe and developing a new one, Boeing executives had made a decision, albeit an implicit one — do nothing — that gradually painted them in a corner. When the A320neo was announced, Boeing chose a route that required a development cycle that was fast, cheap and high quality. Tragically, it failed to meet all three requirements.

1

Introduction

The journey of problem solving

Introduction
—

The journey of problem solving

Let's define *problem* as the gap between where you are and where you want to be. A problem isn't necessarily negative; it can also be an opportunity. At home, you might be deliberating with your spouse whether to buy a house, where to retire, or which car to buy. In a business setting, you might want to select an enterprise-resource-planning platform, decide whether to acquire a competitor, figure out how to respond to a government's threat to erect tariffs, or, indeed, respond to a competitor whose latest plan threatens your market share. Problems are everywhere. We, as individuals and managers in organisations, face them constantly.

This book provides you with a structured process that guides you through the steps to solve complex problems. You will learn to frame your problem, explore potential alternatives, and decide which alternative, on balance, is superior. The book relies on our learnings from teaching this material to hundreds of executives. It provides many hands-on tools such as case studies and, because the immense majority of the problems we face require us to meaningfully engage stakeholders, the book also has **'try this' exercises** that will give you concrete ways to interact with your stakeholders.

In this introductory chapter, you will find out why it's worthwhile to become a good problem solver, why that is not an easy task, and what you can do to develop your problem-solving skills.

GOOD PROBLEM SOLVERS ARE POPULAR . . . BUT HARD TO FIND

From the World Economic Forum to McKinsey, there is widespread agreement that problem-solving skills are of paramount importance.[1] Problem-solving skills often come first on lists of desirable skills, even ahead of other critical ones, such as communication or the ability to deal with ambiguity.

And yet, business education, in particular, does not equip students with good problem-solving skills.[2] It is not surprising, therefore, that employers say it is hard to find people with these capabilities.[3] In short, become a better problem solver and your popularity will shoot up!

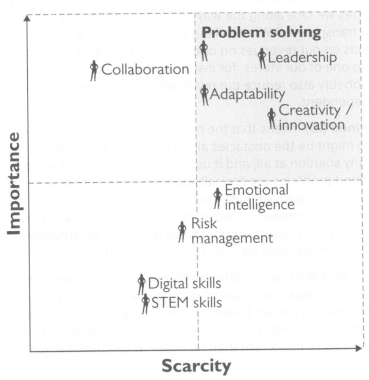

Adapted from (PWC 2017)

SOLVING COMPLEX PROBLEMS IS HARD

If problem-solving skills are in such great demand, why aren't people developing them more? One key reason is that learning to solve the kinds of problems that executives solve – *complex* problems[4] – is hardly a cakewalk. But before we get into that, let's take a step back.

With our definition of a problem (a gap between a current and a desired state), we spend most of our waking hours solving problems, from selecting which socks to wear in the morning to 'betting the farm' on a new strategy. So, there are problems and problems. This book focuses on a subset, so-called CIDNI (pronounced 'seed-nee') problems that are characterised by three defining features:

- **Complex (C)** means that the current and desired states and the obstacles we face along the way are diverse, changing, interdependent, or not transparent.[5] What will our profitability be next year? Well, it depends on our revenues on one side and our costs on the other. Closing one of our stores, for instance, would reduce our costs (yay!) but probably also reduce our revenues, so revenues and costs are interdependent.

- **Ill-defined (ID)** means that the current state and final state are unclear, and so might be the obstacles along the way.[6] The problem may not have any solution at all, and it usually does not have one 'right' solution. Ill-defined problems are typically one of a kind, and what constitutes their best solution is at least partly subjective – yes, we may all agree that we should release a product that is high quality and cheap, but we might assign different importance to these two attributes, thereby causing us to disagree on which solution is best.

- **Non-immediate but important (NI)** means that we don't need a solution right away, we have a few days, weeks, or even months to develop one, so we can follow a systematic process to address the problem. In other words, the quality of the solution we ultimately choose is more important than how fast we end up finding it.

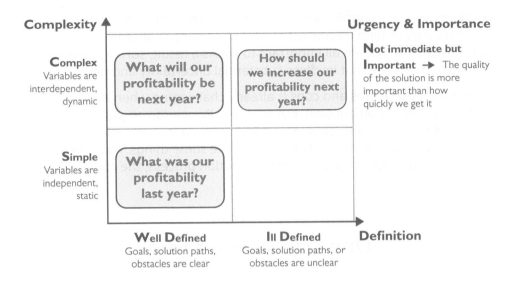

Kate considers various job offers

Kate is a business unit manager at a large multinational consumer goods company, who is facing a challenging career choice. She has been with the company for 15 years and, although successful, she has grown tired of her job. Over the last few months she has explored new opportunities outside the company, which generated three good, but not perfect, offers. As she considers which to choose, she realises that many factors are important to her: the salary, of course, but also opportunities to progress, the quality of her would-be colleagues, and the potential need to relocate. Finally, she needs to bring her fiancé into the decision, because she values his input and because having his support will help her in her new position.

Kate's problem is an example of the CIDNI problems we frequently face at home and at work. Its complexity stems from the interconnectedness of its parts: the job that pays best is outside her preferred region of the world. The challenge is also ill-defined because it's unclear to Kate exactly how much she values opportunities to progress versus the quality of her colleagues, and it's also unclear whether her fiancé will have compatible preferences. Finally, although Kate's challenge is important, she has time to think through it; that is, it is non-immediate.

CIDNI problems[7] typically don't have an obviously superior solution. Instead, they require trading off the pros and cons of alternatives across various criteria that are all important to us. As a result, solving them is a subjective exercise that involves substantial uncertainty and risk.

Trading off these pros and cons is already challenging when we are solving problems on our own, but we typically need to engage various stakeholders – spouses, children, and parents; colleagues, subordinates, and bosses – who are unlikely to all want the same things. As more people need to be integrated into the solution process, the complexity increases.

One size doesn't fit all

Because the complexity of the problems we face varies tremendously, we shouldn't solve them all in the same way.

For many problems, investing in an elaborate solution process makes little sense. Results from one study show that Netflix watchers spend an average of 18 minutes deciding what to watch and that 40% of the people surveyed wanted to watch something different from their significant other[8] (Given these circumstances, 18 minutes actually does not seem so bad!). Having said this, if you conduct such an in-depth analysis every time you select your socks in the morning, your day will grind to a halt before you can say 'paralysis by analysis', all for a small payoff.

Instead, for many problems we're better off relying on routines, habits and intuition. Psychologists call this *System 1* thinking; an automated pathway in our brain that enables us to access lots of data quickly and effortlessly. Using System 1, we make decisions quickly without our conscious minds influencing them. This capability probably evolved when our ancestors were chased by all sorts of long-toothed animals, when it was a literal life saver. There's only so many times that you can ask yourself whether that noise in the nearby bush is from a rabbit or a lion before you get eliminated from the gene pool. Instead, having an automatic 'get-the-heck-out-of-here-now!' function hardcoded in our brain enabled the species to thrive.

For many of our day-to-day decisions, System 1 is the better way to go: It's what enables us to step on the brakes before we hit that car in front of us. We don't need to make a conscious decision, because our intuitive answer usually does a good job, and it does so incredibly fast. It is because we can rely on System 1 thinking for many small decisions that we can get through our days with reasonable efficiency.

However, the speed and relative ease of System 1 thinking comes at a cost: It doesn't care about the quality of the evidence it uses to make the decision. This is particularly relevant as many of today's challenges are probably a lot more complex than those we faced when our neural thinking and decision-making mechanisms came to be.

Most notably, by offering a forceful response to what Nobel laureate psychologist Daniel Kahneman calls WYSIATI (for 'what you see is all there is'), System 1 leaves us vulnerable to various cognitive biases, which pop up time and again as we solve complex problems. Frequent biases include:

- **Confirmation bias**, where we search for and interpret data in a way that confirms our existing beliefs.[9] For instance, when we read the five-star reviews of a restaurant that we are considering but ignore the one-star reviews.

- **Status-quo bias**, where we prefer not to change anything as we perceive all other avenues would be a loss.[10]

- **Bias-blind spot**, where we perceive ourselves to be less biased than others.[11]

- **Anchoring**, where we rely too heavily on the first piece of information considered when making a judgment, even if it's entirely unrelated.[12]

The list goes on. Taxonomies routinely include over 150 biases and even after removing those that significantly overlap, a good 100 remain.[13]

In short, when dealing with complex problems, we can't blindly trust our intuition because it will cause us to fall into many traps. System 1 seems appropriate only in those settings where you're likely to choose a good answer, mistakes have a low cost, and a fast answer is valuable.[14] If these conditions aren't met, however, we'd better consciously initiate a more deliberate, slow, and effort-intensive approach; we need to engage our *System 2 thinking.*

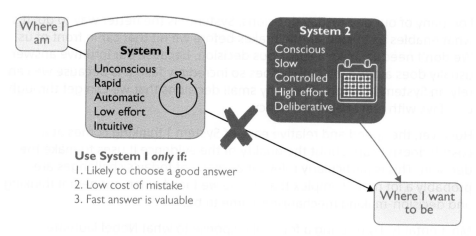

Adapted from Kahneman & Klein, 2009; Evans, 2003; National Research Council, 2011

To be clear, System 2 doesn't guarantee that we won't be unbiased. Completely getting rid of biases is extremely hard and believed by many to not be possible. But engaging System 2 should help us be *less* biased.[15]

To sum up, when facing a complex problem, we must pay attention, which implies that we must slow down. Pretty simple, right? Well, almost. One big difficulty is that System 1 thinking is always running in the background. It is our default approach to dealing with life, so, before we even realise it, we've 'solved' the problem by answering with an expletive that gets us thinking regretfully, 'Did I really just say that?'

Engaging System 2 takes conscious effort. It requires us to Stop. Think. And only then Act. Which is harder than it sounds when we operate in the heat of the moment. Yet, if we don't do it, we let our biases take over with all the negative consequences that doing so might entail.[16]

We fail to solve complex problems in many ways

There are many ways to fall short during the solution process. While helping executives, we see the six listed below particularly frequently.

- **We frame the problem poorly:** Framing the problem means defining what it is and what it is not. Do you really want to increase revenues, or do you want to increase profitability . . . or your return on investment? Although all three frames address the same theme, they don't have the same scope. Framing our effort on increasing revenues, for instance, would leave out reducing costs, whereas framing on increasing profitability would consider both. For complex problems, framing effectively is harder than it appears, because System 1 tells us that we already *know* what the problem is. 'Stop wasting time reviewing useless information' goes the autopilot in our head, 'we know what we want, let's get on with it'. However, there's usually value looking beyond the surface features of a complex problem to validate that what we see is the disease and not just one of its symptoms. That's why Chapters 1, 2, and 3 describe the science and art of framing, enabling you to gain an in-depth understanding of your problem that you can summarise in one overarching key question, your *quest*.

- **We make bad decisions . . . :** In a McKinsey survey, 72% of senior-executive respondents felt that bad strategic decisions in their organisation were at least as frequent as good ones.[17] At some point during the solution process, we need to decide which alternative to pursue, which also means that we need to decide which alternatives *not* to pursue. Yet, making that selection is not trivial. We often see executives entering this stage with preconceptions of what the path forward should be. They spend much of their energy pushing their agenda without seriously exploring alternatives; they ask questions to advocate rather than enquire. As a result, they miss out on solutions that, unbeknownst to them, they might have preferred! Although forcefully plowing ahead gives us the impression that we are getting things done, it might also result in selecting an alternative that we will end up regretting. 'Be careful what you wish for' applies to all of us. Chapter 4 explores how to create better alternatives.

- **. . . or we fail to decide altogether:** If choosing a poor alternative can be disastrous, failing to decide can also be harmful. During the four years before Airbus' announcement of the A320neo, Boeing had been debating whether to update the 737 or start afresh.[18] Not deciding results in perpetuating the status quo, which might lead us to go from a suboptimal position to a downright unacceptable one. Facing uncertainty, we are often tempted to resort to a 'wait and see' attitude. Of course, we don't rationalise it that way; instead we run more analyses, gather more data, engage further with stakeholders, build consensus, . . . and we sometimes miss our window of execution, as Boeing's development of the 737 Max illustrates. Failing to decide is making an (implicit) decision. You'll get practical tools to avoid this trap throughout the book and in particular in Chapters 7 and 9.

- **We don't engage key stakeholders:** Even a solution that seems superior may fail if key stakeholders don't support it. This is especially true when the problem is controversial, with different stakeholders favouring different alternatives. Skilfully engaging these stakeholders makes them co-creators of the end product, thereby increasing the likelihood that they will support the solution.[19] In addition, engaging helps us overcome our own blind spots and biases, as people with different viewpoints, backgrounds, skillsets and agendas are likely to contribute valuable ideas that we might not have.[20] Furthermore, statistically speaking, pooling information from across independent people reduces noise, which results in more reliable information.[21] And being exposed to team decision-making appears to help people make better individual decisions subsequently.[22] Beware, though, as you can have too much of a good thing: under time pressure, for instance, engaging can be counterproductive. Similarly, broad engagement on trivial issues can be perceived as wasteful,[23] and when members in a group already hold an opinion, group discussion can amplify that initial preference.[24] In short, there are times and places where you need to be consultative and other times call for resolute leadership. The point is that you shouldn't consult everyone on every decision but engage judiciously. You will see different ways to engage stakeholders effectively throughout the book.

- **We fail to update our thinking:** Complex problem solving occurs under uncertainty in changing environments, which conflicts with the human need for certainty. As a result, we often form opinions early in the problem-solving process, seek evidence partially, and stick to our opinions, even as new evidence should lead us to revise our conclusions.[25] One key tenet of scientific reasoning is to treat ideas as hypotheses that we test, updating our thinking as we learn.[26] Doing so, we adopt a probabilistic mindset, where we don't see things as right or wrong but we evaluate their probability, which we update when new evidence surfaces. Economist John Maynard Keynes pointed out, 'When the facts change, I change my mind. What do you do, sir?'[27] There is now empirical evidence that adopting such a scientific approach helps in entrepreneurial settings. This book shows you how to develop this mindset, particularly in Chapter 9.

- **We don't execute:** Identifying a good solution is required to solve our problem, but it's not enough. Ultimately, we also need to execute it successfully. Although execution is beyond the scope of this book, we will address this all-important theme throughout.

//// THIS BOOK OFFERS A SOLUTION ////

So, we all face problems of various complexity that call for different solution processes. The simplest problems should be solved with System 1,[28] whereas complex problems call for a more deliberate approach. What's 'more deliberate' then? The last decades have seen the development of a myriad methods to help executives make better decisions. And yet, those are rarely used in the field, arguably because they are often too far removed from practical requirements and too demanding to use.[29]

Solve your problem using FrED

What is needed is an approach that helps safeguard us against our fallible instincts, has the versatility to apply to problems of different degrees of complexity, and remains easy enough to use. We've developed such an approach; we call it FrED:[30]

- **Frame answers: *What is my problem?*** Framing consists of defining the problem, synthesising it into a single overarching key question, the *quest*.

- **Explore answers: *How may I solve my problem?*** Exploring consists of identifying potential answers to the quest – your *alternatives* – and the criteria that will help you decide how much you like each.

- **Decide answers: *How should I solve my problem?*** Deciding consists of identifying which alternative, on balance, you prefer.

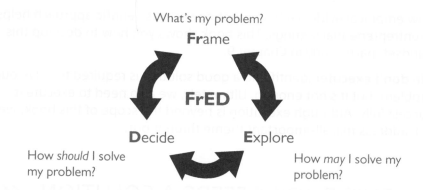

What's my problem?
Frame

FrED

Decide   **E**xplore

How *should* I solve
my problem?

How *may* I solve my
problem?

Think of FrED's three steps as the three legs of a stool. You need all three, as there's only so much that two can do to compensate for a weak third. In other words, to arrive at a good outcome, you can't do a poor job in any of the three steps.

Note as well that framing is problem centric whereas exploring and deciding is solution centric. We all have a tendency to jump quickly to being solution centric (that's our System 1 in action. Yet it pays off to learn to be comfortable being uncomfortable. That is, spend time to better understand the problem; it's okay if we do not have answers right away.

Although FrED's three steps appear linear, in practice you will iterate as new evidence leads you to update earlier conclusions. In fact, rather than starting with framing, problem solving often starts with an idea popping in your head as you take a walk or talk with someone. Nothing wrong with that; with FrED, you can start anywhere and go in any direction!

Dragon Master™, your companion app to solving complex problems

We've developed an app that can help you solve your complex problems. Called Dragon Master™ (for reasons that will become obvious in just a few pages) it enables you to go through the FrED process in one go.

Dragon Master™ is free and accessible at dragonmaster.imd.org

Don't let FrED's simplicity deceive you. It is immensely versatile, applying to whichever challenge you face, no matter what its nature. We've used it to help people solve problems in disciplines as varied as business strategy, particle physics, medicine, architecture, and philosophy. You can adapt its granularity to match your circumstances, simply using it as a mental roadmap if you need to organise your thinking on the fly all the way down to structuring a multi-year project.

Tested and refined over hundreds of projects, FrED has shown it promotes problem solving in two major ways. First, it helps you provide clear direction to yourself, your team and your organisation about what you'll do. Second, it helps you engage your key stakeholders better. As we'll see, it is critical to do both: provide direction and engage stakeholders. If you only provide direction (adopting 'my way or the highway' as a motto), you are likely to lose your stakeholders along the way. Similarly, a pure focus on engagement (thinking 'let a 1,000 flowers bloom') puts you at risk of ineffectively investing your limited resources. That's why the book continuously moves back and forth between these two poles.

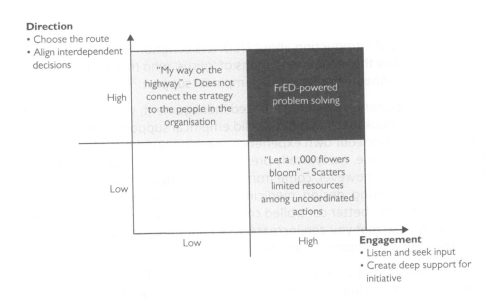

Direction
- Choose the route
- Align interdependent decisions

High — "My way or the highway" – Does not connect the strategy to the people in the organisation | FrED-powered problem solving

Low — | "Let a 1,000 flowers bloom" – Scatters limited resources among uncoordinated actions

Low | High — **Engagement**
- Listen and seek input
- Create deep support for initiative

By providing an overarching structure to organise your problem-solving effort, FrED is like an operating system. Much like Windows or MacOS, it provides a stable underlying platform on which you can run specialised analyses – financial, marketing, or supply chain analyses – that are required to solve your problem. More specifically, FrED allows you to gain systematic insights into your problem that help you go beyond your intuition while remaining simple to apply.

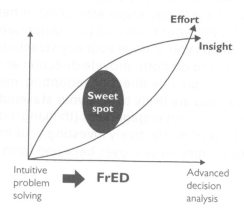

One final point of introduction about FrED. It is common in managerial settings to follow the recommendations of 'gurus' who make arguments that sound reasonable but have little empirical support.[31]

As strong proponents of evidence-based management, we have strived to include in this book ideas that have solid empirical support. Some of this support comes from our own experience coaching hundreds of executives. When that's the case, we typically present the source as 'in our experience'. Most of the ideas, however, come from a body of literature in the social sciences, engineering, design, medicine, and other disciplines that have been tested under better controlled conditions. We have strived to indicate these sources so that you can increase your confidence in the findings that have the stronger empirical support.[32]

One of these sources of empirical findings is the Crew Resources Management (CRM) literature. Over the past few decades, the aviation industry has taken unprecedented steps to improve how airline crews make decisions, steps that have coincided with a drastic drop in fatalities.[33] The CRM literature centralises these learnings, providing a strong body of empirically derived knowledge that is getting adopted in other areas, including the maritime and the healthcare industries.[34]

Because CRM practices leverage an optimal set of characteristics – centralised reporting systems of accidents, systematic investigation of accidents, development and testing of prescriptive rules, and so on – we believe they provide high-quality evidence that can help decision making in other settings, including managerial ones. As a result, we call on this body of knowledge extensively throughout the book.

In the end, however, the applicability of any finding to another setting depends on the validity of the original finding and on its capacity to be validly transposed to the new setting. Although we believe that the ideas we present score well on both counts, we strongly encourage you to engage your critical thinking and test each claim for yourself.

How to use this book

Mimicking FrED's structure, the book has three parts: frame, explore, decide.

Part I, Frame, describes the science and art of framing, enabling you to gain an in-depth understanding of your problem that you summarise in one overarching key question, your *quest*. More specifically, Chapter 1 lays out how to define your quest and contextualise it by introducing a hero, a treasure and a dragon. Chapter 2 shows how to fine-tune your hero-treasure-dragon-quest sequence by using four rules. Then, Chapter 3 helps you sharpen your understanding even further by exploring the problem's underlying root causes.

Part II, Explore, sets the stage for exploring potential alternatives and criteria to solve your problem. Chapter 4 shows how to explore the solution space which results in concrete alternatives, using *how* maps. Chapter 5 helps you explore, articulate and weigh relevant decision criteria that will help you identify the most promising alternatives.

Part III, Decide, builds on the work that you have done in the first two parts, to help you make well thought-out decisions. Chapter 6 lays out how to evaluate and compare alternatives using a weighted set of criteria. Chapter 7 shows how to make interdependent decisions across multiple domains of choices. Chapter 8 shows how to summarise your conclusions in a compelling message to win the support of your key stakeholders. Finally, Chapter 9 helps you move forward under uncertainty, showing you how to adopt a probabilistic mindset suited to complex situations and linking the strategising that you have done throughout the journey with the execution still ahead.

As you read through the chapters, relating the ideas and tools to your challenge, don't hesitate to skip back and forth between different chapters. FrED is best used as an iterative process where insights from one step help you modify the conclusions you have reached in previous steps.[35] Don't look at this as a failure but as a welcome progress towards being less wrong, towards reaching better conclusions.

In practice, we have found it useful to go through the whole book once to understand the bigger picture before deep diving into the chapters that best address the most important issues you face. In parallel, the dedicated Dragon Master™ app will help you capture your thinking at all three stages of the process.

/////////// CHAPTER TAKEAWAYS ///////////

Problem solving is bridging the gap between where you are and where you want to be. As such, we constantly solve all sorts of problems.

CIDNI problems are particularly relevant. 'CIDNI' stands for complex, ill-defined, non-immediate but important. In the following, we shorthand CIDNI problems as simply *complex*.

For simple problems, following our intuition (System 1 thinking) is fine. For complex problems, however, intuition is dangerous because it makes us particularly vulnerable to various biases. Instead, we should be more deliberative, engaging System 2 thinking.

One way to engage System 2 thinking is to use a three-step approach to solve complex problems: FrED.

- **Frame answers: *What is my problem*?** Framing consists of defining the problem, synthesising it into a single overarching key question, the *quest*.

- **Explore answers: *How may I solve my problem*?** Exploring consists of identifying potential answers to the quest – your *alternatives* – and the criteria that will help you decide how much you like each.

- **Decide answers: *How should I solve my problem*?** Deciding consists of identifying which alternative, on balance, you prefer.

///////// INTRODUCTION NOTES /////////

1 For WEF reference, see page 22 of World Economic Forum (2016). The future of jobs: Employment, skills and workforce strategy for the fourth industrial revolution. Global Challenge Insight Report, World Economic Forum, Geneva. For McKinsey reference, see *McKinsey Quarterly* (2020). Five fifty: Soft skills for a hard world. National Research Council (2011). Assessing 21st century skills: Summary of a workshop.

2 Bunch, K. J. (2020). 'State of undergraduate business education: A perfect storm or climate change?' *Academy of Management Learning & Education* **19**(1): 81–98.

3 See page 44 of PWC (2017). The talent challenge: Harnessing the power of human skills in the machine age.

4 There's no unified definition of what a complex problem is. For discussions, see Dörner, D. and J. Funke (2017). 'Complex problem solving: what it is and what it is not.' *Frontiers in Psychology* **8**: 1153.

5 See, for instance, p. 5 of Mason, R. O. and I. I. Mitroff (1981). *Challenging strategic planning assumptions: Theory, cases, and techniques*, Wiley New York. See pp. 87–90 of Mason, R. O. (1969). 'A dialectical approach to strategic planning.' *Management Science* **15**(8): B-403-B-414; Wenke, D. and P. A. Frensch (2003). "Is success or failure at solving complex problems related to intellectual ability?" *The psychology of problem solving*. J. E. Davidson and R. J. Sternberg. New York, Cambridge University Press: 87–126.

6 See p. 4 of Pretz, J. E., A. J. Naples and R. J. Sternberg ibid. Recognizing, defining, and representing problems: 3-30; see p. 462 of Smith, S. M. and T. B. Ward (2012). Cognition and the creation of ideas. *Oxford handbook of thinking and reasoning*, Oxford: 456–474.

7 For brevity, we'll refer to CIDNI problems from now on as *complex problems*.

8 Goldman, R. and C. Gilmor (2016). New study reveals we spend 18 minutes every day deciding what to stream on Netflix. *IndieWire*.

9 See, for instance, Nickerson, R. S. (1998). 'Confirmation bias: a ubiquitous phenomenon in many guises.' *Review of General Psychology* **2**(2): 175–220.

10 See, for instance, Kahneman, D., J. L. Knetsch and R. H. Thaler (1991). 'The endowment effect, loss aversion, and status quo bias.' *Journal of Economic Perspectives* **5**(1): 193–206.

11 Pronin, E., D. Y. Lin and L. Ross (2002). 'The bias blind spot: Perceptions of bias in self versus others.' *Personality and Social Psychology Bulletin* **28**(3): 369–381.

12 Anchoring is tricky. Tversky and Kahneman's 1974 experiment is a classic example of anchoring. They generated a random number between 0 and 100 before asking participants to decide whether the percentage of African countries in the UN was above or below that number. Anchoring was exposed when the participants' median estimate was larger when the random number was high than when it was low. See Tversky, A. and D. Kahneman (1974). 'Judgment under uncertainty: Heuristics and biases.' *Science* **185**(4157): 1124–1131.

13 For a taxonomy, see Dimara, E., S. Franconeri, C. Plaisant, A. Bezerianos and P. Dragicevic (2018). 'A task-based taxonomy of cognitive biases for information visualization.' *IEEE Transactions on Visualization and Computer Graphics* **26**(2): 1413–1432. See also Yagoda, B. (2018). 'The cognitive biases tricking your brain.' *The Atlantic* (September).

14 See p. 79 of Kahneman, D. (2011). *Thinking, fast and slow.* New York, Farrar, Straus and Giroux. See also Milkman, K. L., D. Chugh and M. H. Bazerman (2009). 'How can decision making be improved?' *Perspectives on Psychological Science* **4**(4): 379–383. For biases more specific to decision and risk analysis, see Montibeller, G. and D. Von Winterfeldt (2015). 'Cognitive and motivational biases in decision and risk analysis.' *Risk Analysis* **35**(7): 1230–1251.

15 See, for instance, Lawson, M. A., R. P. Larrick and J. B. Soll (2020). 'Comparing fast thinking and slow thinking: The relative benefits of interventions, individual differences, and inferential rules.' *Judgment & Decision Making* **15**(5).

16 Debiasing is hard. Kahneman, for one, is dubious that it can be done, and research has shown that merely knowing about a bias doesn't prevent us from succumbing or make us aware that we have it (Pronin, E., D. Y. Lin and L. Ross (2002). 'The bias blind spot: Perceptions of bias in self versus others.' *Personality and Social Psychology Bulletin* **28**(3): 369–381). However, some ways have been proposed (Soll, J. B., K. L.

Milkman and J. W. Payne (2015). A user's guide to debiasing. *The Wiley Blackwell handbook of judgment and decision making*. G. Keren and G. Wu.) and recent research provides evidence that some training might help. See Morewedge, C. K., H. Yoon, I. Scopelliti, C. W. Symborski, J. H. Korris and K. S. Kassam (2015). 'Debiasing decisions: Improved decision making with a single training intervention.' *Policy Insights from the Behavioral and Brain Sciences* **2**(1): 129–140. Sellier, A.-L., I. Scopelliti and C. K. Morewedge (2019). 'Debiasing training improves decision making in the field.' *Psychological Science* **30**(9): 1371–1379.

17 We make bad decisions. Adopting a process perspective, a bad decision is the result of an unsystematic decision-making process, or to be more precise, a decision process that bypasses one or more of FrED's steps. See Enders, A., A. König and J.-L. Barsoux (2016). 'Stop jumping to solutions!' *MIT Sloan Management Review* **57**(4): 63. See De Smet, A., G. Lackey and L. M. Weiss (2017). 'Untangling your organization's decision making.' *McKinsey Quarterly*: 6980. (De Smet, A., G. Jost and L. Weiss (2019). 'Three keys to faster, better decisions.' *The McKinsey Quarterly*.) Management scholar Denise Rousseau identifies six organisational biases that lead to poor decisions. These overlap significantly with our own observations (slightly revised): solving the wrong problem, ignoring politics, considering just one alternative, focusing on a single criterion, narrow interests dominate, over-relying on easily available evidence. Rousseau, D. M. (2018). 'Making evidence-based organizational decisions in an uncertain world.' *Organizational Dynamics*.

18 Campbell, D. (2019). 'Redline: The many human errors that brought down the Boeing 737 Max.' *The Verge* **9**. See also Clark, N. and J. Mouawad (2010). Airbus to update A320 with new engines and wings. *The New York Times*. Polek, G. (2011). Boeing takes minimalist approach to 737 Max. *Aviation International News*; Peterson, K. and T. Hepher (2011). Race is on for sales of Boeing's MAX vs Airbus neo. *Reuters*. Hemmerdinger, J. (2021). 'How and why Boeing re-engined the 737 to create the Max.' *FlightGlobal*. Campbell, D. (2019). 'Redline: The many human errors that brought down the Boeing 737 Max.' *The Verge* **92**019. *The Guardian* (2020). Boeing 737 Max readies for takeoff after EU signals safety approval is imminent. Gelles, D., N. Kitroeff, J. Nicas and R. R. Ruiz (2019). Boeing Was 'Go, Go, Go' to Beat Airbus With the 737 Max. Herkert, J., J. Borenstein and K. Miller (2020). 'The Boeing 737 MAX:

Lessons for engineering ethics.' *Science and Engineering Ethics* **26**(6): 2957–2974. Smith, A., J. Maia, L. Dantas, O. Aguoru, M. Khan and A. Chevallier (2021). Tale spin: Piloting a course through crises at Boeing. *IMD Case 7-2279.*

19 This tendency of people to value things that they contributed to create is sometimes called the IKEA effect. See Norton, M. I., D. Mochon and D. Ariely (2012). 'The IKEA effect: When labor leads to love.' *Journal of Consumer Psychology* **22**(3): 453–460.

20 See, for instance, Pronin, E., T. Gilovich and L. Ross (2004). 'Objectivity in the eye of the beholder: Divergent perceptions of bias in self versus others.' *Psychological Review* **111**(3): 781. Pronin, E., J. Berger and S. Molouki (2007). 'Alone in a crowd of sheep: Asymmetric perceptions of conformity and their roots in an introspection illusion.' *Journal of Personality and Social Psychology* **92**(4): 585.

21 Ariely, D., W. Tung Au, R. H. Bender, D. V. Budescu, C. B. Dietz, H. Gu, T. S. Wallsten and G. Zauberman (2000). 'The effects of averaging subjective probability estimates between and within judges.' *Journal of Experimental Psychology: Applied* **6**(2): 130. Johnson, T. R., D. V. Budescu and T. S. Wallsten (2001). 'Averaging probability judgments: Monte Carlo analyses of asymptotic diagnostic value.' *Journal of Behavioral Decision Making* **14**(2): 123–140.

22 Maciejovsky, B., M. Sutter, D. V. Budescu and P. Bernau (2013). 'Teams make you smarter: How exposure to teams improves individual decisions in probability and reasoning tasks.' *Management Science* **59**(6): 1255–1270.

23 De Smet, A., G. Jost and L. Weiss (2019). 'Three keys to faster, better decisions.' *The McKinsey Quarterly.*

24 This is called *group polarization*; see, for instance, Sunstein, C. R. (1999). 'The law of group polarization.' University of Chicago Law School, *John M. Olin Law & Economics Working Paper*(91).

25 See Samuelson, W. and R. Zeckhauser (1988). 'Status quo bias in decision making.' *Journal of Risk and Uncertainty* **1**(1): 7–59.

26 We fail to update our thinking. Bayesian updating, a.k.a. updating one's thinking in light of new evidence, is central to FrED, so we'll talk

more about it. For the benefit of scientific thinking in entrepreneurial settings, a recent study found that entrepreneurs who had trained in defining clear hypotheses, rigorously testing them, and deciding based on the results of the tests achieved significantly better results than others who didn't get the same training; see Camuffo, A., A. Cordova, A. Gambardella and C. Spina (2020). 'A scientific approach to entrepreneurial decision making: Evidence from a randomized control trial.' *Management Science* **66**(2): 564–586.

27 This quote is attributed to John Maynard Keynes with some controversy, as there are also sources that list economist Paul Samuelson as having coined a similar phrase. See Kay, J. (2015). 'Keynes was half right about the facts.' *Financial Times* **4**.

28 System 1 and System 2 thinking. The terms were coined by psychologists Keith Stanovich and Richard West (Stanovich, K. E. and R. F. West (2000). 'Individual differences in reasoning: Implications for the rationality debate?' *Behavioral and Brain Sciences* **23**(5): 645–665.) and adopted by Kahneman (see pp. 20–28 of (Kahneman, D. (2011). *Thinking, fast and slow*. New York, Farrar, Straus and Giroux.). To learn more, Barbara Spellman's introduction is a great primer (Spellman, B. A. (2011). *Individual reasoning. Intelligence analysis: Behavioral and social scientific foundations*. C. Chauvin and B. Fischhoff, National Academies Press). Kahneman's Nobel lecture (Kahneman, D. (2002). 'Maps of bounded rationality: A perspective on intuitive judgment and choice.' *Nobel Prize Lecture* **8**: 351–401) offers a more detailed summary. For yet more, see Kahneman (2011).

29 Riabacke, M., M. Danielson and L. Ekenberg (2012). 'State-of-the-art prescriptive criteria weight elicitation.' *Advances in Decision Sciences* **2012**, ibid.

30 FrED comes from everywhere. We developed FrED based on our experience having worked with hundreds of executives and integrating the problem-solving approaches of multiple academic disciplines including the scientific hypothesis-driven approach (Gauch, H. G. (2003). *Scientific method in practice*, Cambridge University Press.), the TRIZ methodology in engineering, (Ilevbare, I. M., D. Probert and R. Phaal (2013). 'A review of TRIZ, and its benefits and challenges in practice.' *Technovation* **33**(23): 30–37) and the design thinking way of, well, designers and the methods used by top strategy consultancies (Davis, I., D. Keeling, P. Schreier and A. Williams (2007). 'The McKinsey approach to problem solving.' *McKinsey Staff Paper* **66**).

31 Don't trust the gurus! In medical settings, the opinion of experts is the lowest-grade evidence. For more, see for instance, Galluccio, M. (2021). Evidence-informed policymaking. *Science and diplomacy*, Springer: 65–74), Ruggeri, K., S. van der Linden, C. Wang, F. Papa, J. Riesch and J. Green (2020). 'Standards for evidence in policy decision-making.'

32 For more on this practice see, for instance, p. xxii of Barends, E., D. M. Rousseau and R. B. Briner (2014). Evidence-based management: The basic principles, Amsterdam.

33 Pasztor, A. (2021). The airline safety revolution: the airline industry's long path to safer skies. *The Wall Street Journal*.

34 See, for instance, Helmreich, R. L. (2000). 'On error management: Lessons from aviation.' *British Medical Journal* **320**(7237): 781–785. Haerkens, M., M. Kox, J. Lemson, S. Houterman, J. Van Der Hoeven and P. Pickkers (2015). 'Crew resource management in the intensive care unit: A prospective 3-year cohort study.' *Acta Anaesthesiologica Scandinavica* **59**(10): 1319–1329. Wahl, A. M. and T. Kongsvik (2018). 'Crew resource management training in the maritime industry: A literature review.' *WMU Journal of Maritime Affairs* **17**(3): 377–396. Helmreich, R. L., J. A. Wilhelm, J. R. Klinect and A. C. Merritt (2001). 'Culture, error, and crew resource management.' Haerkens, M. H., D. H. Jenkins and J. G. van der Hoeven (2012). 'Crew resource management in the ICU: The need for culture change.' *Annals of Intensive Care* **2**(1): 1–5.

35 FrED is iterative. See Rittel's wicked problems (Rittel, H. W. (1972). 'On the planning crisis: Systems analysis of the "first and second generations".' *Bedriftsokonomen* **8**: 390–396). FrED has friends. Our process is just one of many to help decision making and problem solving. Others include DODAR (Diagnosis, Options, Decide, Assign Tasks, Review) and FOR-DEC (Facts, Options, Risks and Benefits—Decide, Execute, Check) from the aviation industry (see p. 167 of Orasanu-Engel, J. and K. L. Mosier (2019). Flight crew decision-making. *Crew resource management*. B. G. Kanki, J. Anca and T. R. Chidester. London, Academic Press: 139–183); OODA (Observe, Orient, Decide, Act); and many others. Woods identified 150 strategies used in many disciplines (Woods, D. R. (2000). 'An evidence based strategy for problem solving.' *Journal of Engineering Education* **89**(4): 443–459).

Part I

FRAME – Understand your problem

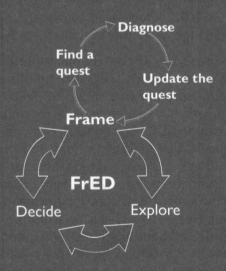

Remember you need the following components to solve your problem[1]:

- The overarching question that summarises your problem – the *quest*
- Various *alternatives* to answer that question
- *Criteria* that will help you identify which of these alternatives you prefer
- The *evaluations* of each alternative on each criterion.

Framing helps you get to that first piece, the quest. Developing a good frame is harder than it looks. It is usually best achieved as an iterative process. To guide you, Chapter 1 helps you identify an initial quest and contextualise it. Chapters 2 and 3 help you enhance the frame by fixing any misalignments and refining your quest.

Through this journey you will likely realise that, at the outset, you only have a superficial understanding of your problem. This is a common pitfall – and a dangerous one. Fixing a symptom is often much less effective than fixing the cause of the pain. To sidestep this trap, Chapter 3 will show you how to diagnose your problem – that is, identify its root causes – and use these insights to improve your quest.

By the end of Part I, you will know how to synthesise your problem in a clear and concise frame that includes a protagonist (the *hero*), a goal that the hero wants to achieve (the *treasure*), an obstacle between the two (the *dragon*) and the key question you want to address (the *quest*) (see below).

A good frame is clear and concise

Hero: Solveable Media provides marketing services to the US health care industry; its revenues have been constant for the last five years. I am the CEO of Solveable Media.

Treasure: I want to increase Solveable Media's revenues by 10% annually over the next five years.

Dragon: However, Solveable Media's current sales force doesn't have enough people.

Quest: How can I increase Solveable Media's revenues by 10% annually over the next five years, given that Solveable Media's current sales force doesn't have enough people?

Chapter One

Define your quest – Create an initial frame

Framing your problem means articulating what your problem is. To help you do so, a frame provides with three main parts: (1) a substance part; (2) an engagement part (with information on the stakeholders involved); and (3) a logistics part. Let's get started on the first part.

Borrowing from archetypical narratives in storytelling, you can capture the substance of the problem by summarising it in a single overarching question, the *quest*, that you contextualise with a clearly defined protagonist (the *hero*),

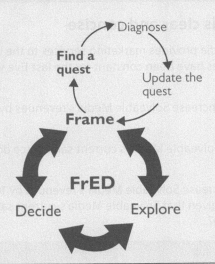

a goal that the hero wants to achieve (the *treasure*), and an obstacle between the two (the *dragon*).

The managers and executives we work with often start seeking solutions without having properly framed the challenge they face. 'We know what we want', they think, 'so let's not waste time on framing. *I* am in the business of getting things done'. Sensible approach! After all, nobody wants to get to a solution more slowly than needed.

Yet, like it or not, how a problem is framed matters (see below).[2] People tend to underappreciate what they don't know, and poor framing partly explains why a large proportion of strategic decisions fail.[3] First, if you frame poorly, you risk addressing a symptom, or a perceived problem, rather than the underlying disease.[4] Consider a patient who goes to the doctor because of a headache. The doctor might prescribe an aspirin, which will mask the pain. This is fine if the headache results from too much partying the night before, but if our patient's headache is only a symptom of a bigger problem, say, a tumour, treating the symptom might lead to disastrous results down the line. That's why physicians conduct proper diagnoses before prescribing, a practice that we recommend adopting for managerial problems.

Framing matters

Two monks, addicted to smoking, often debated whether it was sinful to smoke during prayers. Eventually they decided to independently approach the abbot to ask him and met afterwards to discuss the outcome.

The first monk reported a disastrous meeting: The abbot had refused his request and had given him extra penance to do. 'What did you ask the abbot?' asked monk #2. 'I asked him if it was OK to smoke while praying.'

'Funny', said monk #2, 'I had a great meeting: The abbot granted my request to smoke and commended me on my worthy attitude!' 'Good God', gasped monk #1, 'But, what did you ask?'

'I asked him if it was OK to pray while smoking.'[5]

Second, poor framing also creates problems when you ask your stakeholders to support your conclusions. If you haven't considered their perspectives in your framing, expect struggles when 'selling' them on the merits of your approach.

An effective frame is also critical because you know more than your stakeholders. Working on your problem for days, weeks or months, you will easily presume that they know more than they do. We often see this perception gap, called the *curse of knowledge,* between project teams and their stakeholders. In 1990, Elizabeth Newton, a psychology PhD student at Stanford, conducted an experiment where she separated a group of people into 'tappers' and 'listeners'. Tappers had to pick a well-known song, such as *Let it be* or *Happy birthday,* and tap out the rhythm with their fingers on the table, while the listeners had to guess the name of the song. The success rate was abysmally low: Only 2.5% of the 120 songs that were tapped out were guessed correctly. The twist is that prior to tapping out the song, Newton had asked the tappers what the probability was that the listeners would guess correctly. They predicted that 50% would get it right.[6] You wonder why they were so overconfident? Well, try out the tapping game yourself. It's hard to imagine that someone else won't be able to identify a song when you hear it play in your head.

Of course, an intuitive response to the blank stare of our counterpart is to tap harder. Does this remind you of what happens in some team meetings when people don't manage to make themselves understood? Being aware of this curse is a good reminder that what appears obvious isn't necessarily so. Luckily a good frame can help.

So, how do we start framing? Research and our experience with hundreds of executives show that using stories can help.[7] In particular, well-told stories are easy to comprehend, because events causally relate to one another; they are interesting, because of the tension they create and resolve; and they are easy to remember, because of their causal structure.[8] You can frame your problem by summarising it in the form of a story that has a protagonist (the *hero*), an aspiration (the *treasure*), and an obstacle between the two (the *dragon*). Putting these three elements together creates a *quest*: how should [the hero] get [the treasure], given [the dragon]?

////////// FIND YOUR QUEST //////////

A good way to frame is to start from the end – with the quest. The quest is the *one* overarching question that your solution efforts aim to answer. Once you answer your quest, you have a clear strategy for moving forward, and 'all' that's left is to implement it.

Phrase your quest as an open question that starts with *how*. Closed questions can be answered in a binary yes/no manner; for instance: Should we invest in this IT project? In contrast, open questions help us consider more alternatives: How should we invest to improve our IT infrastructure? Every now and then, it might be judicious to start your quest with *what* but, in our experience, these cases are extremely rare. These *what* questions as well as other open questions – *who, where, when* – can usually be formulated as *how* questions (for instance, 'what is the best strategy to increase our revenues by 10%?' can be rephrased as 'how should we increase our revenues by 10%?').

The great thing about a well-phrased quest is that answering it provides a clear strategy.[9] Answering the quest tells us what needs to be implemented – instead of yielding other questions that require further analysis. For instance, if you want to improve your company's profitability, 'how can we increase our profitability?' is an appropriate quest, but 'how do customers buy our products?' isn't, because answering it would only yield an intermediary step, not a solution.

Although this approach is extremely powerful, it hinges on the quest being 'well-phrased', which is why we devote much effort to phrasing our quest carefully.

Examples of quests from the executives we have worked with are wide ranging, including:

- How should we increase sales for product X, given that they have dropped over the past two years?

- How should we enter market Y, given that we would face well-entrenched competitors?

- How should I progress in my career, given that I have high costs to cover?

To help you write a good quest, focus on three key characteristics: its type, its scope, and its phrasing of the question.

- A good *type* means that answering the quest yields potential solutions; it doesn't just lead to more analysis. To help you do so, start your quest with a 'how' (instead of *why*, *who*, *what*, or *where*).

- A good *scope* means that the quest is neither too narrow nor too broad.

- Finally, good *phrasing* means that the quest is self-contained and easily understandable even by a novice when reading it once.

Out of these three characteristics, finding a good scope for your quest can be particularly challenging. Not convinced? Let's see. What quest do you think that our friend Charles, in the drawing below, has set for himself? You may want to pause for a minute and write it down. Writing it down is actually important, because it helps you be accountable, so we strongly advise you to take the extra seconds to do it!

When we ask this question in class, participants often answer, 'how do I make my door safe?' We agree. This is probably the quest that he has set for himself, but is this the quest that he should have set for himself? Clearly not, because the weak point in his house isn't the door, it's the window. So maybe Charles should ask 'how do I make my house safe?' But why stop there? Why not ask 'how do I make my life safe?' or, for that matter, 'how do I make my life better?'

There are obvious implications to choosing the scope of your quest. Choose too narrow a scope and you risk being ineffective, missing the problem altogether. Choose too wide a scope and you risk being inefficient, dedicating limited resources to addressing issues that add little value. Your objective is to be somewhere in between these two extremes, with an appropriate scope.[10]

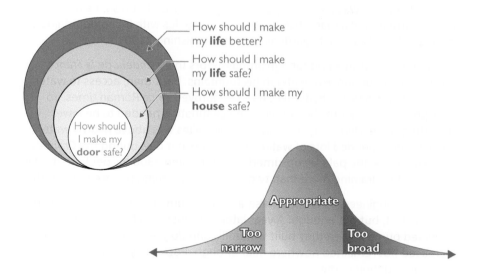

Taking into account Charles' challenges in scoping a quest, take a minute to think about a first quest for one of the complex challenges that you are facing. How broad or narrow should it be? Which elements should be included and which ones left out to make it comprehensive yet manageable? Take a first informed guess, and remember that you will be able to further refine your quest throughout the rest of the FrED process. In short, don't aim for perfection, but get things started. To help you, here are a few more ideas.

Be attentive to weak signals

Think of taking off for a long-distance flight, say from Mumbai to Rome. Any deviation in your heading during the first moments of the flight might lead you to Algiers or Moscow a few hours later. The same logic applies to your project: If you orient yourself poorly at the outset, you will probably not end up where you'd like. In other words, in a quest, every word counts (see box 'Framing matters' above).

Louis XIV is *really* thirsty – or why in framing the quest, every single word matters[11]

In 1661, Louis XIV was 23 and eager to show his power. To do so, he ordered the construction of a magnificent palace in Versailles with lots of fountains. At its peak, Versailles and its gardens had an astonishing 2400 fountains.

The king enjoyed showing foreign ambassadors the *grandeur de la France* through the abundance of water in his fountains. Back then, access to water was a luxury. However, hydraulics hadn't improved since Roman times. To transport water, we only had gravity; the destination needed to be lower than the source. Herein lay the problem; Versailles was above nearby water sources and it needed lots of water. Three hours per day, during the *Grandes Eaux* spectacle, the palace consumed an astonishing 6300 m^3 per hour (that is equivalent to draining more than two Olympic swimming pools every hour!).

So, in 1662, engineers installed a horse-activated pump that brought 600 m^3/day. A good start, but not enough. A year later, they installed bigger horse-activated pumps. Then they built windmills and dug reservoirs. The capacity increased but remained nowhere near enough. Pushed by Louis, the engineers upped their game.

In 1668, they rerouted the Bièvre river and added more windmills. Seven years later, they built a 1500m-long aqueduct. Fountains could now operate several hours per day and Versailles was using more water than Paris. Yet, it was still not enough.

So, engineers proposed to pump water up from the Seine River. It was bold, considering that the river was ten kilometres away . . . and 140 m *below* Versailles. They created the gargantuan Machine de Marly, which entailed diverting part of the Seine with two dams and building the machine, a complex system with 14 enormous wheels, each 11 metres in diameter, that powered 220 pumps taking water 165 metres high. The effort required 1800 workers, took three years, and cost an astonishing 5.5m livres (€750m in today's money). Dubbed the most complex machine of the seventeenth century, it required 60 people to operate. Its theoretical capacity was 3200 m^3/day, which was astonishing . . . but still not enough.

So, the quest for water continued. In 1680, the king's engineers dug lakes and interconnected them with a 34 km artificial river and in 1685, work started on an 80 km-long long canal. The project was pharaonic – 30,000 men worked on it! Alas, in 1689, France was at war against the League of Augsburg and was going bankrupt. Work on the aqueduct stopped; it would never resume.

Bringing water to Versailles ended up costing one third of building the palace. Despite their best efforts, engineers never brought enough water.

So, how did Versailles operate the fountains without enough water? What worked where 30,000 men and a pharaonic budget failed?

Whistling. Instead of operating fountains continuously, the king's fountaineers whistled. Upon hearing a colleague whistle, a fountaineer knew that the king was getting close to his fountain. He would then quickly open up the water flow, enabling the king to point out the beautiful waterworks to the mesmerised ambassadors accompanying him. All it took was for the fountaineers to warn his next colleague with a brief whistle and cut off the water in his own fountain the moment that the king's party was out of sight.

Getting enough water to Versailles was a problem that engineers never fully cracked as they focused on answering: *How should we bring sufficient water to the king's fountains?*

But what if, instead, they had asked: *How should we bring sufficient water for the king's fountains to achieve their desired effect?*

The two questions are nearly similar, yet they lead to vastly different solutions, illustrating that in a frame, every single word counts.

In practice, we shouldn't delegate framing to our autopilot (our System 1 thinking) but continuously check that we address what we *actually* want to achieve (System 2 thinking), which requires us to be attentive to weak signals.

Auto racing legend Juan Manuel Fangio mastered weak signal detection. Fangio qualified first in the 1950 Formula One Monaco Grand Prix and therefore started the race in pole position. Powering through the first curves, he didn't realise that nine cars behind him had crashed, creating a pileup that blocked the road. Soon he came around the track, fast approaching the crash site hidden by a blind corner, when he noticed yellow flags waving, a sign to be cautious. What really caught Fangio's attention though was a much subtler sign. 'I came to the harbour front and I could detect agitation among the spectators. They were not looking at me leading the race, but were looking the other way. I braked very hard' he said, instinctively raising his hand as a warning sign to following drivers.[12] Fangio went on to win that day and eventually collected five World Championship titles; an unprecedented feat at a time when Formula One accidents were often lethal and careers cut short by horrific accidents.

For Fangio, detecting weak signals while racing a Formula One car down the narrow streets of Monaco was a matter of life and death. Fortunately, most of us don't operate under such unforgiving conditions, and we don't need to be nearly as good. Still, detecting weak signals is useful when framing complex problems. Re-reading a quest, we might get a nagging feeling that something is odd. Maybe it's not saying exactly what we'd like it to say, even though we can't quite articulate what is off. This is a weak signal, and the tools that you will acquire in this chapter and the next will sharpen your ability to detect them.

All of this takes effort, so it is tempting to bypass developing a good quest. Don't. Because whatever efforts you invest early in the solution process can pay huge dividends.

Decision-making happens throughout the process

Your problem framing sets the stage for decision-making.[13, 14] In theory, we get to deciding after framing the problem and exploring alternatives and criteria, in the form of a climax where the fundamental components of the process – the quest we're addressing, the alternatives we've created, the criteria that matter to us, and the evaluations of each alternative on each criterion – come together.[15] Part III of the book covers this step of the process, discussing in detail how to make thoughtful decisions. In practice, however, deciding doesn't just happen in the third step of FrED. Rather, deciding permeates the entire process.

When framing, you need to decide what your quest is and what it is not. You also need to contextualise it, deciding what belongs in that frame. At this stage, you already make critical decisions, including which stakeholders to onboard onto your problem-solving team, which to consult, which to inform, and which to leave out.

Then you need to decide how to deploy your limited resources during the problem-solving process. Should you conduct a full-blown diagnosis or take the risk to bypass it? How extensive should you make your search for alternatives? How many of these alternatives should you formally evaluate? What criteria should you include and how should you weigh them? What analysis is needed to evaluate the alternatives? How will you craft your recommendations? All these decisions profoundly affect your analysis, so let's look at how to be thoughtful about making them – particularly those affecting your frame.

//// DON'T AUTOMATICALLY USE THE FIRST QUEST THAT //// COMES TO MIND

Odysseus (or Ulysses in English), a legendary Greek king of Ithaca and the hero of Homer's epic poem, wanted to hear the sirens' songs, but he knew he wouldn't be able to resist them. So he ordered his men to tie him to the ship's mast to prevent him from jumping overboard, to put wax in their ears to protect them from the songs, and to keep the ship's course no matter what. Conscious of his limitations, Ulysses took pre-emptive measures.

To this day, a Ulysses contract enables the contractor to bind herself in the future to a pre-set course of action if she suspects she might be unwilling or unable to do so on her own volition.[16] Ulysses' tale illustrates what research has shown: such commitment devices can be effective ways to help us protect against our imperfect selves.[17] Given how tempting it is to quickly jump into solving the problem before even understanding it, we need to tie ourselves to the ship's mast. Therefore, if, like Ulysses, you doubt that you can resist the lure of jumping to a solution prematurely, make your own Ulysses contract by considering various quests before committing to one, which you can do in a diverge–converge sequence:

- **Step 1 – Diverge:** First, to consider various quests, you may want to ask colleagues co-solving the problem with you to each identify two to five possible quests *independently*. You may do so with brainwriting, which research has shown is often more effective than brainstorming.[18] To do so, ask everyone to write at least two potential quests – two because it's frequent for everyone to think about more or less the same quest by default; so if you only ask for one, you might get little diversity of ideas. Ask them to do their initial thinking independently, by writing down their answers, to avoid contaminating others' thinking (see the anchoring bias in Introduction). You may then collect the answers and circulate them for everyone to generate a second round of ideas. For the Odysseus contract part, commit to not progress before going through, say, at least three rounds or dedicating one hour to the exercise. In other words, give yourself licence to diverge in your thinking.

- **Step 2 – Converge:** Second, to focus on the best quest, compare the potential quests: What are their benefits and drawbacks? Are there some that you can eliminate? Could you combine various into one? Once you are reasonably happy with your preferred quest, write it down and move to the next step – contextualising it.

Identifying a quest is an important milestone, because you have reduced your problem to a single question. Now is a great time to take stock: Would answering that quest give you a strategy that, coupled with skilful execution, is likely to solve your problem? If so, fantastic, you're off to a great start! If not, you may want to invest a little more in this step.

//// CONTEXTUALISE YOUR QUEST ////

Now that you have identified a worthy quest, contextualise it by putting it into a concise frame, using the Hero-Treasure-Dragon-Quest sequence. The *hero* includes all the important information needed to introduce the part of the universe of interest, including the main protagonist, who might be a single individual – in fact, it's usually you! But the hero can also be a group of people – a team or an organisation. In movie parlance, the hero is the establishing shot. Strive to include as little information as possible but as much as needed. Let's see how that works in Louis' challenge of bringing water to his Versailles palace.

> **Hero**: In the 1660s, King Louis XIV is building the palace of Versailles with hundreds of fountains, which he wants to use for his own entertainment and for impressing foreign dignitaries. I and five colleagues ('we') work for Louis XIV as water engineers.

In this example, the hero is the team of water engineers, *not* Louis (which, had he known, might have been devastating to him, being the Sun King and all).

Next, present the hero's aspiration, the one overriding goal that she wants to achieve, be it financial success, market expansion, world peace, or a happy life. That aspiration is the *treasure.* In our example, the treasure might be:

> **Treasure**: We want to bring sufficient water for the king's fountains to produce their desired effect.

Note that at this stage all is well in your story. With the hero and treasure, you have only shown the part of the universe that you want to focus on. In screenwriter Robert McKee's words, a story 'begins with a situation in which life is relatively in balance'. Things are good, and daily activities occur more or less how the people of interest want them to.[19]

In other words, there is no problem yet! Equally important, there is nothing that reasonable people who are familiar with your issue would dispute. Everything is more or less as we would expect. One simple way to check that your [hero + treasure] is non-problematic is to validate that it doesn't contain any 'but' or 'however'. Another check is to envision yourself presenting it to your key stakeholders. Would everyone nod in agreement, or would there be pushback? If so, you probably need to iron out a few things.

Now, any good story with a hero and a treasure also needs a *dragon*. The dragon is the obstacle that prevents the hero from getting the treasure. In storytelling, a dragon is the inciting event that throws life out of balance. To clearly surface this tension, introduce your dragon with 'however'. All was well in the universe ([hero + treasure]); *however*, a dragon is throwing a wrench in the works, so to speak.

Dragon: However, it is difficult to bring sufficient water to Versailles.

The dragon creates the tension in the frame that will be the launch pad for your problem-solving efforts. If there is no dragon, there is no tension, and therefore no problem to solve!

For any problem, there are many potential dragons, so consider various ones before selecting the one that creates the most relevant tension for you and your key stakeholders.

Deal with multiple dragons

You will often find yourself in a position where you have more than one problem. Costs might be spiralling out of control, *and* the sales team might not be performing well, *and* your technology platform is outdated. In other words, you are facing multiple dragons; let's call those baby dragons (see below).

There are two ways of dealing with baby dragons. One is to find an umbrella problem that summarises all of the baby dragons – the big dragon. You can then write the frame with that big dragon. Solving your problem would take you one FrED process with that big dragon at the centre of the frame.

Alternatively, you can separate the problem into smaller ones. You would then write a frame for each baby dragon giving each its own FrED process. That means that you would have various quests, one for each baby dragon. Like movie sequels. But, just as sequels aren't released at the same time, this second approach typically means that you will address the baby dragons one at a time, in separate problem-solving efforts. Irrespective of the approach you choose, remember the unicity requirement: it's *one* hero, *one* treasure, and *one* dragon; otherwise it's more than one story.[20]

Phil sorts out his baby dragons

Phil participated in one of our programs at IMD. He was unsure how to formulate his frame. 'The problem I would like to tackle is: Should I invest time, money, and energy in starting my own business and if so, what business should I start? This problem has two parts: Should I start a business and, if so, what type of business.' Phil is entirely correct, he is asking two questions, which violates our unicity requirement.

Phil's statement could be turned into a single question: 'How should I start my own business, given that I am concerned about the associated risk, money and time commitment?' However, this framing does not address whether Phil should be starting a business in the first place. As Phil pointed out: 'I'm not sure if this new framing captures the essence of the problem, especially the element of "should I do it in the first place?". Likewise, I'm not sure if my two-part challenge – should I do it and if so, how should I do it – can be combined effectively into one, or if it should be separated into two challenges.'

But it doesn't have to be that way. Upon further exploration, Phil found a quest that included both elements: 'How should I invest my next five to ten professional years, given that I'm not realising my life's dream in my current role?'

Summarising his dragons in a single statement – 'I'm not realising my life's dream in my current role' – enabled Phil to clean up his thinking while setting up the ground for evaluating the trade-offs of each potential path forward.

Summarise your problem in a single overarching question: your quest

Bringing together the hero, treasure, and dragon, we inevitably get back to our quest, which is best expressed as, 'How should [the hero] get [the treasure], given [the dragon]?' For Louis' engineers, the quest might be:

Quest: How can we deliver enough water to the king's fountains to keep him happy, given that it is difficult to bring water to Versailles?

Other examples of quests include:

- How should our business unit increase sales, given that our sales team is underperforming?

- How should we enter the Chinese market, given that we don't have any experience in international expansion?

- How should we stop our fiercest competitor from entering our core market, given that they are operating with a business model that is much more low cost?

- How should Dave Calhoun return Boeing to success as a leading aircraft manufacturer, given that the 737 Max crisis has drastically reduced trust in Boeing?

- How should I invest my next five to ten professional years, given that I'm not realising my life's dream in my current role?

The above quests span a wide range of topics that, on the surface, look unique. If you don't look beyond these surface features, addressing them requires starting your solution process from scratch each time, which increases the effort needed and decreases the probability that

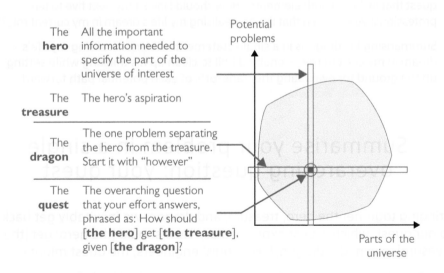

The | All the important
hero | information needed to specify the part of the universe of interest

The | The hero's aspiration
treasure

The | The one problem separating the hero from the treasure.
dragon | Start it with "however"

The | The overarching question that your effort answers,
quest | phrased as: How should [**the hero**] get [**the treasure**], given [**the dragon**]?

Potential problems

Parts of the universe

you can adapt innovative ideas you've seen elsewhere to that new problem.

On the other hand, if you learn to recognise commonalities across problems – in their structure or in the solution process – you will drastically improve your abilities to solve even problems you know nothing about. So there is value in framing problems in a consistent manner to make similarities more noticeable. One way to do that is to formulate your quests with a consistent structure: 'How should [the hero] get [the treasure], given [the dragon]?'[21]

At this stage, you might want to take a crack at framing your problem. Below is a template to fill out your Hero-Treasure-Dragon-Quest (HTDQ) sequence. You can use it here, or head over to the Dragon Master™ app (accessible at dragonmaster.imd.org) and frame your problem there.

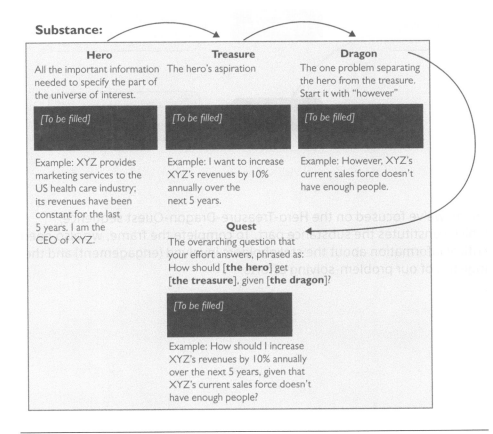

/// COMPLETE THE FRAME: DEFINE /// ENGAGEMENT AND LOGISTICS

Recall that a good frame has three parts: substance, engagement, and logistics.

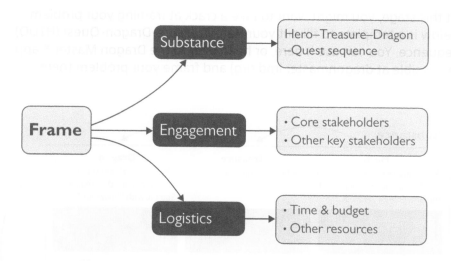

So far, we've focused on the Hero-Treasure-Dragon-Quest sequence, which constitutes the substance part. To complete the frame, we also need critical information about the stakeholders involved (engagement) and the logistics of our problem-solving efforts.

Identify the stakeholders

Flying planes used to be the business of the captain, assisted by the first officer and, in the old days, the flight engineer. Over the last five decades, however, the aviation industry has redefined what it considers a crew to account for the fact that, at times, flight attendants, dispatchers, fuellers, loaders, gate agents, and ground crews can all provide information that is unavailable in the cockpit. Although the captain remains in charge of decisions, one of her critical responsibilities is to decide *whom* to involve and *when* to do so to make the best possible decision.[22]

But if engaging more and different people can help, more engagement isn't *necessarily* better as it can lead to wasted time.[23] As a leader, you simply can't consult everyone for every issue without paralysing the organisation. So, whom should you engage when?

To start, it's useful to identify two sets of stakeholders:

- **Core stakeholders** are the people co-solving the problem with you and those with formal decision power on the process or its outcome. They include the individual(s) responsible for making the decision, who 'own the problem'.[24]

- **Other key stakeholders** are the people who aren't actively involved in the solution process but who are impacted by it or who can influence the success of the solution.

With limited resources, you might be inspired to engage these groups differently, being more active with core stakeholders. In our experience, it is useful to listen more than you speak, so that you can understand their perspectives, which might translate into new ideas. Also, when you are speaking, don't just share *what* you propose to do but also *why* you think so, to help them understand how you reached your conclusions.

It might be useful as well to assign roles to the people you engage judiciously, giving some a chance to opine, others an actual vote, others still a formal veto.[25]

Who is your PM?[26]

Airline captains are trained to create environments where crew members feel comfortable asking questions, stating opinions, and challenging authority when necessary. To promote these behaviours, captains learn to, as early as possible in the flight, create opportunities for crew members to provide information and use these opportunities to praise the person.

In addition, crew members are trained to speak up no matter what environment the captain creates. This behaviour goes hand-in-hand with a re-thinking of the role of the first officer. In the old days, the captain was king with full power of decision, the pilot flying (PF) and the co-pilot was the pilot not flying (PNF). This denomination has lately been replaced by PM, for 'pilot monitoring', implying that even if not flying the plane, the PM is an active participant in crew operations with a shared responsibility for the safe conduct of the flight. The PM has many responsibilities to support the pilot flying, but chief among those is to observe the PF's performance to detect any threat. To promote this sharing of responsibilities, pilots are evaluated as crew.

If you are the PF in your problem solving, who is the PM who has your back?

Sort out the logistics

The last part of the frame is to spell out the logistics of your effort, identifying how much time, money, and other resources you are ready to dedicate to it. Committing this information in writing forces you to think it through. It also helps document your position at the onset of the effort, knowing that it might evolve along the project but that it should evolve as the result of a conscious decision. Finally, it helps create shared understanding across the team – what psychologists call a shared mental model (SMM) – which has been shown to support team effectiveness.[27]

Below is a template for capturing this information.

Engagement:

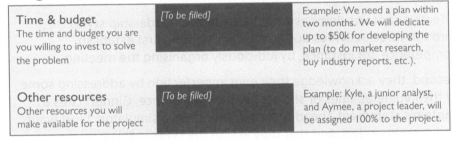

Core stakeholders The people co-solving the problem with you and those with formal decision power on the process or its outcome (e.g. your boss, your client)	*[To be filled]*	Example: XYZ's chief marketing officer (CMO) will co-solve.
Other key stakeholders The people not actively involved in the process but who are impacted by it or can influence the project	*[To be filled]*	Example: YZ's current sales team. XYZ's C-suite executives (beside the CMO).

Logistics:

Time & budget The time and budget you are you willing to invest to solve the problem	*[To be filled]*	Example: We need a plan within two months. We will dedicate up to $50k for developing the plan (to do market research, buy industry reports, etc.).
Other resources Other resources you will make available for the project	*[To be filled]*	Example: Kyle, a junior analyst, and Aymee, a project leader, will be assigned 100% to the project.

////////// ASK FOR HELP //////////

Daniel Kahneman and Dan Lovallo highlight the dangers of considering problems from the inside-out perspective, where we treat each as a one-off.[28] Instead, they suggest that we adopt an outside-in approach, where we treat the problem as an instance of a broader group.[29] Enlisting others might help you do that, as they will bring different perspectives. Others will also see your blind spots better than you can.

Seeking candid external opinions requires creating a space where people are encouraged to disagree, so that issues are vigorously debated. Research in how effective airline crews do so might be a good guide (see box below).

Create a safe space like an exemplary airline captain

Errors that are shared by some or all of the members of a team might stem from a failure to detect, a failure to indicate, or a failure to correct.[30]

Airline crews sometimes meet for the first time only minutes before working together, and these pre-flight briefing sessions set the tone for the team interactions.[31] Leadership specialist Robert Ginnett analysed how effective airline captains establish a safe space.

Effective captains demonstrate their adaptive leadership styles through three activities during pre-flights. They first establish competence, for instance, by judiciously organising the meeting.

Second, they acknowledge their own imperfection by addressing some of their vulnerabilities or shortcomings. For instance, Ginnett cites a captain's statement ahead of a crew session in a simulator, 'I just want you guys to understand that they assign the seats in this airplane based on seniority, not on the basis of competence. So anything you can see or do that will help out, I'd sure appreciate hearing about it.'

And third, effective captains engage the crew by modifying the meeting in real time to integrate elements that emerge during it. This enables them to show that their authority is flexible and dependent on the situation.[32]

A good frame looks simple, which is immensely useful because you can present your problem to anybody – including people who know nothing about it – in just a few phrases. Getting to that simplicity, however, isn't trivial. You must think through the various aspects of your problem, pitching different perspectives against one another, and deciding which information belongs in your frame. Just like any craft, it takes hard work and experience to make a frame look easy. Chapter 2 gives additional guidelines to improve your craft.

/////// CHAPTER TAKEAWAYS ///////

We all have a tendency to go straight into solution mode, looking for great answers . . . but starting by asking better questions is a valuable investment. Before jumping to solutions, invest in framing your problem.

Any complex problem can be summarised into a single key question or *quest*. A good quest has an appropriate type, scope, and phrasing.

Furthermore, the quest is part of a broader structure that captures the substance of the problem clearly and succinctly: The Hero-Treasure-Dragon-Quest (HTDQ) sequence:

- **The hero** includes all the important information needed to introduce the part of the universe of interest, including the main protagonist, who might be a single individual, a team, or an organisation. Strive to include as little information as possible but as much as needed.

- **The treasure** is the hero's aspiration.

- **The dragon** is the one problem separating the hero from the treasure. Start it with 'however'.

- **The quest** contains the overarching question that your effort answers. It typically takes the form: How should [*the hero*] get [*the treasure*], given [*the dragon*]?

A project has *one* hero, *one* treasure, *one* dragon, and *one* quest. Nothing Nothing more – the unicity principle.

Don't be like Louis! Realise that, in a quest, a few words can mean the difference between 30,000 men digging a canal 80 km long and two dozens of fountaineers whistling.

Tie yourself to the mast. If, like Odysseus, you doubt that you will be able to resist the lure of flying to solutions, protect yourself by identifying various quests, comparing them, and selecting the best.

Like world champion Fangio, be attentive to weak signals; in the frame, make every word count. Read your Hero-Treasure-Dragon-Quest sequence out loud. If you feel that you need to deviate from what's written, maybe you're not quite there yet.

Don't fool yourself, it's easy to believe that one is the sole owner of the truth, but reality usually paints a different picture. Consulting actively with your stakeholders can provide a good reality check.

In short, be methodical, but don't overstress it either. The next chapter will give you more tools to finesse your Hero-Treasure-Dragon-Quest sequence.

////////// CHAPTER 1 NOTES //////////

1 The components of decisions. We focus on four key components: the quest, alternatives, criteria, and evaluations. For an alternative model, see p. 430 of Matheson, D. and J. E. Matheson (2007). From decision analysis to the decision organization. *Advances in decision analysis – From foundations to applications*. W. Edwards, R. F. J. Miles and D. von Winterfeldt, Cambridge: 419–450; and p. 39 of Howard, R. A. and A. E. Abbas (2016). *Foundations of decision analysis*, Pearson Education Limited.

2 For a discussion, see Bach, D. and D. J. Blake (2016). 'Frame or get framed: The critical role of issue framing in nonmarket management.' *California Management Review* **58**(3): 66–87.

3 See Walters, D. J., P. M. Fernbach, C. R. Fox and S. A. Sloman (2017). 'Known unknowns: A critical determinant of confidence and calibration.' *Management Science* **63**(12): 4298–4307. Poor framing partly explains . . . Paul Nutt (1999). 'Surprising but true: Half the decisions in organizations fail.' *Academy of Management Perspectives* **13**(4): 75–90) singled out three major reasons to explain why half of the decisions in organisations fail: managers pressure teams to limit the search for alternatives, imposing their solutions, and using power to implement plans. As for problem framing, Nutt observes: 'defining a problem is a familiar way for managers to initiate decision making. Managers want to find out what is wrong and fix it quickly. The all too frequent result is a hasty problem definition that proves to be misleading. Symptoms are analyzed while more important concerns are ignored.' For empirical evidence that better framing is associated with better results in entrepreneurial settings, see Camuffo, A., A. Cordova, A. Gambardella and C. Spina (2020). 'A scientific approach to entrepreneurial decision making: Evidence from a randomized control trial.' *Management Science* **66**(2): 564–586.

4 This is sometimes called a Type III error; see pp. 180–181 of Clemen, R. T. and T. Reilly (2014). *Making hard decisions with DecisionTools*, Cengage Learning.

5 Adapted from *Irish Times* (1997). Pope's fancy footwork may have saved the life of Galileo.

6 For more on the study, see Elisabeth Newton's dissertation with the description of the tapping game – pp. 33–46 of Newton, E. L. (1990). *The rocky road from actions to intentions*. Stanford University. For more on the curse of knowledge/curse of expertise, see, for instance, Camerer, C., G. Loewenstein and M. Weber (1989). 'The curse of knowledge in economic settings: An experimental analysis.' *Journal of Political Economy* **97**(5): 1232–1254; Hinds, P. J. (1999). 'The curse of expertise: The effects of expertise and debiasing methods on prediction of novice performance.' *Journal of Experimental Psychology: Applied* **5**(2): 205; Keysar, B., L. E. Ginzel and M. H. Bazerman (1995). 'States of affairs and states of mind: The effect of knowledge of beliefs.' *Organizational Behavior and Human Decision Processes* **64**: 283–293; Keysar, B. and A. S. Henly (2002). 'Speakers' overestimation of their effectiveness.' *Psychological Science* **13**(3): 207–212; and Heath, C. and D. Heath (2006). 'The curse of knowledge.' *Harvard Business Review* **84**(12): 20–23.

7 Gershon, N. and W. Page (2001). 'What storytelling can do for information visualization.' *Communications of the ACM* **44**(8): 31–37.

8 See P. 66–67 of Willingham, D. 'Why Don't Students Like School?: A Cognitive Scientist Answers Questions About How the Mind Works and What It Means for the Classroom' 2010, Jossey Bass.

9 Ask three strategy professors for their definition of strategy and you'll likely get five answers! So, for the sake of clarity, here's our definition: A strategy is a plan of action to achieve an overall objective.

10 For more on breadth of frames, see pp. 46–47 of Wedell-Wedellsborg, T. (2020). *What's your problem?*, Harvard Business Review Press.

11 Bibliothèque Nationale de France. (2015). 'Le château de Versailles, 1661–1710 – Les fontainiers.' Retrieved 11 May, 2021, from http://passerelles.bnf.fr/techniques/versailles_01_6.php.

12 Williamson, M. (2011). 'Fangio escapes the pile-up.' **2020** (June 7).

13 See also Bhardwaj, G., A. Crocker, J. Sims and R. D. Wang (2018). 'Alleviating the plunging-in bias, elevating strategic problem-solving.' *Academy of Management Learning & Education* **17**(3): 279–301 and Chevallier (2019). 'A rock and a hard place at RWH.' *Case IMD-7-2186*.

14 Create an environment that supports participatory decision-making. Collaborative decision-making specialist Sam Kaner advises that you should encourage all to speak their mind; promote the understanding of one another's needs and goals and accept their legitimacy; find solutions that are inclusive of all, not just the most vocal stakeholders; and agree that all are responsible for designing and managing the process that results in the decision. See Kaner, S. (2014). *Facilitator's guide to participatory decision-making*, John Wiley & Sons, p. 24.

15 Keeney, R. L. (1992). *Value-focused thinking: A path to creative decisionmaking*. Cambridge, Massachusetts, Harvard University Press; Howard, R. A. and J. E. Matheson (2005). 'Influence diagrams.' *Decision Analysis* **2**(3): 127–143.

16 Spellecy, R. (2003). 'Reviving Ulysses contracts.' *Kennedy Institute of Ethics Journal* **13**(4): 373–392. See also pp. 200–203 of *Duke, A. (2018). Thinking in bets: Making smarter decisions when you don't have all the facts*, Portfolio.

17 Ariely, D. and K. Wertenbroch (2002). 'Procrastination, deadlines, and performance: Self-control by precommitment.' *Psychological Science* **13**(3): 219–224.

18 Thinking independently: Brainwriting has been shown to yield better results than brainstorming. See, for instance, pp. 109–111 of Rogelberg, S. G. (2018). *The surprising science of meetings: How you can lead your team to peak performance*, Oxford University Press, USA. See also Heslin, P. A. (2009). 'Better than brainstorming? Potential contextual boundary conditions to brainwriting for idea generation in organizations.' *Journal of Occupational and Organizational Psychology* **82**(1): 129–145; Linsey, J. S. and B. Becker (2011). Effectiveness of brainwriting techniques: comparing nominal groups to real teams. *Design creativity 2010*, Springer: 165–171; and Kavadias, S. and S. C. Sommer (2009). 'The effects of problem structure and team diversity on brainstorming effectiveness.' *Management Science* **55**(12): 1899–1913. For a discussion of the comparative merits of brainstorming and brainwriting, and the Delphi method, see pp. 125–128 of Chevallier, A. (2016). *Strategic thinking in complex problem solving*. Oxford, UK, Oxford University Press. See also Keeney, R. L. (2012). 'Value-focused brainstorming.' *Decision Analysis* **9**(4): 303–313.

19 McKee, R. and B. Fryer (2003). 'Storytelling that moves people.' *Harvard Business Review* **81**(6): 51–55.

20 We deep dive into this important point in Chapter 7.

21 Another way is to learn to recognise similarities in problems that look nothing like one another. We'll discuss this technique, called analogical problem solving, in Chapter 4.

22 The captain assembles the team. See p. 53 of Tullo, F. J. (2019). Teamwork and organizational factors. *Crew resource management*, Third edition. London, Elsevier: 53–72.

23 See De Smet, A., G. Jost and L. Weiss (2019). 'Three keys to faster, better decisions.' *The McKinsey Quarterly*.

24 See pp. 11–12 of French, S., J. Maule and N. Papamichail (2009). *Decision behaviour, analysis and support*, Cambridge University Press.

25 See, for instance, the RAPID approach for assigning roles in Rogers, P. and M. Blenko (2006). 'Who has the D.' *Harvard Business Review* **84**(1): 52–61.

26 See pp. 54–58 of Tullo, F. J. (2019). Teamwork and organizational factors. *Crew resource management*, Third edition. London, Elsevier: 53–72.

27 Dijkstra, F. S., P. G. Renden, M. Meeter, L. J. Schoonmade, R. Krage, H. Van Schuppen and A. De La Croix (2021). 'Learning about stress from building, drilling and flying: a scoping review on team performance and stress in non-medical fields.' *Scandinavian Journal of Trauma, Resuscitation and Emergency Medicine* **29**(1): 1–11.

28 Kahneman, D. and D. Lovallo (1993). 'Timid choices and bold forecasts: A cognitive perspective on risk taking.' *Management Science* **39**(1): 17–31. See also p. 117–121 of Tetlock, P. E. and D. Gardner (2015). *Superforecasting: The art and science of prediction*, Random House.

29 Outside-in approach. Kahneman and Lovallo's suggestion (Kahneman, D. and D. Lovallo (1993). 'Timid choices and bold forecasts: A cognitive perspective on risk taking.' *Management Science* **39**(1): 17–31) echoes a comment by novelist Salman Rushdie: 'the only people who see the whole picture are the ones who step out of the frame.'

30 Sasou, K. and J. Reason (1999). 'Team errors: definition and taxonomy.' *Reliability Engineering & System Safety* **65**(1): 1–9.

31 See p. 171 of Orasanu, J. (2010). Flight crew decision-making. *Crew resource management.* B. G. Kanki, R. L. Helmreich and J. Anca. San Diego, CA, Elsevier: 147–180.

32 See pp. 100–102 of Ginnett, R. C. (2010). 'Crews as groups: Their formation and their leadership.' *Crew resource management.* B. Kanki, R. Helmreich and J. Anca: 79–110. See also Lingard, L., R. Reznick, S. Espin, G. Regehr and I. DeVito (2002). 'Team communications in the operating room: Talk patterns, sites of tension, and implications for novices.' *Academic Medicine* **77**(3): 232–237. See also p. 307 of Rogers, D. G. (2010). 'Crew Resource Management: Spaceflight resource management.' *Crew resource management.* B. G. Kanki, R. L. Helmreich and J. Anca. San Diego, CA, Elsevier: 301–316.

Chapter Two
—
Fine-tune your quest – Improve your frame

Chapter 1 gave you ideas to develop a basic frame. Now, let's look at how to improve it.

Statistician George Box famously said, 'all models are wrong, but some are useful'. What he meant was that a model is, by design, a simplification of reality. Useful models, then, are useful simplifications: they only retain what's critical, omitting everything else.

Think of your frame as a model. Instead of capturing everything about your problem, a judicious frame balances simplicity and accuracy. When developing your frame, your job is to make things as simple as possible, but no simpler. Following the four rules below will help you do that.

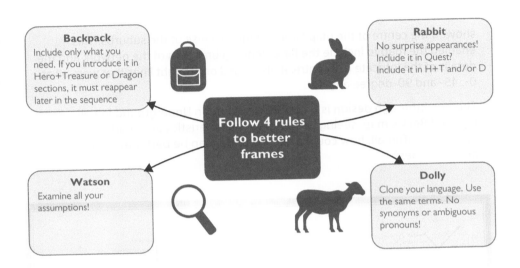

Backpack
Include only what you need. If you introduce it in Hero+Treasure or Dragon sections, it must reappear later in the sequence

Rabbit
No surprise appearances! Include it in Quest? Include it in H+T and/or D

Follow 4 rules to better frames

Watson
Examine all your assumptions!

Dolly
Clone your language. Use the same terms. No synonyms or ambiguous pronouns!

TRAVEL LIGHT – THE BACKPACK RULE

More information is better. Right? Well, not so fast. Research has shown that, in problem solving, less is often more.[1] Not only that, but we often don't realise that, to improve something, we might be better off *removing* things than adding some.[2] And yet, just as a more exact map isn't necessarily more useful (see below), or a product with more features isn't necessarily better,[3] the most detailed frames are *not* necessarily the best. In fact, in our experience, concise frames are almost always much, much better.

Mr. Beck's map[4]

In 1931, electrical draftsman Harry Beck drew a map of the London Underground.

Until then Tube maps were all based on the surface geography, but Beck's design introduced drastic changes in support of making the map easier to read. For one, his map wasn't drawn to scale. Its purposely distorted geometry showed the centre of the map larger, at the expense of the suburbs. This enabled the map to include the far-extending branches of the network and the details of the intricate city centre. It also relied on straight lines that were all at 0-, 45- and 90-degree angles.

The breakthrough design is probably why London Underground initially rejected Beck's map, seeing its defining characteristics as a mark of inferiority; after all, how could a less accurate map be better than more accurate ones?

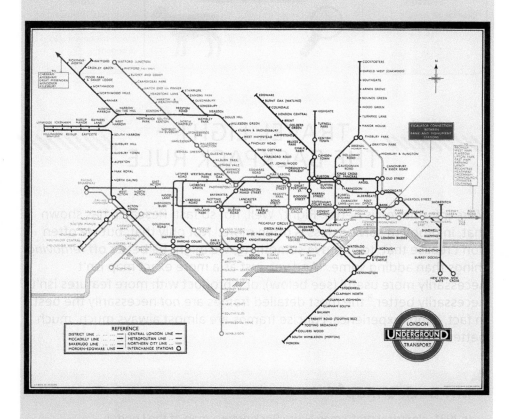

But during a trial run, users enthusiastically adopted Beck's map, which became the official map of the London tube and the blueprint for representing underground systems the world over.

Attempting to pack too much information into a frame is one of the most common and detrimental pitfalls we encounter. Time and again we see even seasoned executives present massive amounts of information in slides labelled 'background' with no clear reason why it is shown (see below).

Jerry gives too much information

Jerry, a sales manager for a large insurance company, participated in one of our programmes. He wanted to help his company sell more policies to millennial clients. During the project kick-off, his task was to introduce his challenge to the other programme participants in two minutes. He started by talking about the company's history, told his peers about how re-insurance processes worked, and went into details about the company's org chart and its successes and failures expanding internationally. During his expansive introduction, he kept buying a little more attention from his audience by telling them: 'Bear with me, this is all important background information.' As he ran out of time, Jerry hurriedly introduced his quest, which focused on making his company be more present on social media – something that he had not mentioned until then.

Jerry's presentation was well structured; he had clearly segmented each part of his presentation. But as he introduced wave after wave of information, most of which only contained only peripheral details, he drowned his audience, whose most polite members were trying to continue to swim along while most others were checking their emails. Jerry's frame had far too much information. He had brought a satellite photo to navigate the London Tube and, in doing so, he left his audience scratching their heads wondering: 'Where is he going with all of this?'

Of course, giving background information to your audience is important, but that doesn't give you licence to throw everything and the kitchen sink at them, expecting them to sort out what is relevant and what is not in real time while you present. Instead, *you* must decide what to show, very much like Beck did with the London Tube map. Crafting a frame, then, entails making decisions, which management scholar Richard Rumelt aptly captures, noting that 'an important duty of any leader is to absorb a large part of [the] complexity and ambiguity, passing on to the organization a simpler problem—one that is solvable'.[5]

So, how do you avoid overfilling your frame? The *backpack rule* reminds you to include just what you need. It states that all *meaningful* information in one part of the frame must appear again at least once in another part.[6] If, in the hero, you mention that your company's revenues have been stable for the last ten years, you need to pick this up later, in the treasure, the dragon or the quest. Otherwise, that information probably doesn't belong to the frame.

The backpack rule takes its name from the careful selection process you (should!) undergo as you prepare for a long hike. You'd better plan carefully what you take along, because you will need to carry all of it throughout your adventure. One of us (Albrecht) vividly remembers one tour through the Swiss Alps where he brought a camping cooker that he ended up not using even once. But boy, was it heavy! So, pack as light as possible: bring everything you'll need, but nothing that you won't.

	Without the rule	With the rule
H+T	I work in NYC as the general manager of a startup. **We create software for kids to learn maths. We started with local kids, but we've seen a lot of traction in the UK and we've also found potential investors in the UK.** I want to go to London for a business trip.	I work in NYC as the general manager of a startup. I want to go to London for a business trip.
D	However, I don't know how I should go to London.	However, I don't know how I should go to London.
Q	How should I go from NYC to London for a business trip, given that I don't know how to go there? ✗	How should I go from NYC to London for a business trip, given that I don't know how to go there? ✔

Backpack
Include only what you need. If you introduce it in *H+T* or *D*, it must reappear later in the sequence

Effective frames work the same way – put in everything that is necessary, but no more. In essence, the backpack rule is a reformulation of the second half of Chekhov's gun principle, named after Russian playwright Anton Chekhov, that states that 'if a gun is clearly visible on the mantelpiece for two acts [of a play], it had better go off during the third'.[7]

AVOID SURPRISE APPEARANCES– THE RABBIT RULE

Coined by philosopher Neil Thomason, the rabbit rule is the mirror image of the backpack rule. It highlights that a magician cannot pull a rabbit out of a hat without first putting the rabbit in the hat.[8] The same applies in frames. Everything in your quest must have already appeared earlier in the frame; there are no late surprise appearances!

Note that Chekhov had also thought about this, as he advised 'if you have a gun going off in the third act of a play, it had better sit on the mantelpiece during the first two acts'.

In Jerry's presentation (see above), the challenge for the audience was not just staying afloat among the packets of information coming at them. It was also that Jerry's quest had a rabbit – being more present on social media – that had not appeared before, which confused the group even further.

The simplicity of the Hero-Treasure-Dragon-Quest sequence enables the executives we work with to quickly check if they follow the backpack and rabbit rules. They almost invariably find that their sequence needs a little (or a lot of!) streamlining but that this effort is well spent as it sharpens their understanding of the problem.

	Without the rule	With the rule
H+T	I work in NYC as the general manager of a startup.	I work in NYC as the general manager of a startup.
	I want to go to London.	I want to go to London for a **business trip**.
D	However, I don't know how I should go to London.	However, I don't know how I should go to London.
Q	How should I go from NYC to London for a **business trip**, given that I don't know how to go there? ✗	How should I go from NYC to London for a **business trip**, given that I don't know how to go there? ✔

Rabbit

No surprise appearances! Include it in Q? Include it in H+T and/or D

CLONE YOUR LANGUAGE – //// THE DOLLY-THE-SHEEP RULE ////

Dolly was the first mammal successfully cloned. Applying the Dolly rule means referring to things in the same way throughout the frame rather than using synonyms or ambiguous pronouns.

The Dolly rule can be a little counterintuitive! We often see executives working on their frame rehashing memories of their English 101 college class where they were told not to be repetitive. But in problem solving, using synonyms for describing the same thing may confuse your audience. So, don't try to create a literary masterpiece out of your Hero-Treasure-Dragon-Quest sequence. Instead, aim for simplicity, clarity, and brevity. If that gets it to be branded boring by some, so be it. Besides, if it's brief enough, they won't have time to get bored!

	Without the rule	With the rule
H+T	I work in NYC as the general manager of a startup.	I work in NYC as the general manager of a startup.
	I want to go to **London** for a business trip.	I want to go to **London** for a business trip.
D	However, I don't know how I should go to **the UK**.	However, I don't know how I should go to **London**.
Q	How should I go **overseas** for a business trip, given that I don't know how to go there?	How should I go from NYC to **London** for a business trip, given that I don't know how to go there?

✗ ✔

Dolly
Clone your language. Use the same terms. No synonyms or ambiguous pronouns!

Note that you might feel compelled to refer to something in two different manners. When that happens, in addition to cursing Dolly, ask yourself why you feel compelled to use different terms. This introspection will likely help you gain additional insight into your problem, exposing a detail that you hadn't considered up to now.

//// EXAMINE YOUR ASSUMPTIONS – //// THE WATSON RULE

In 2014, the French rail operator SNCF ordered 341 new trains at a cost of €15 billion. A few years later, when the trains started to be delivered, the company realised that they were too wide for some 1300 platforms at train stations across the country. Altering those came at a cost of another €50 million.[9] The source of this costly and embarrassing mistake was that the engineers who designed the trains relied on the measures of platforms built less than 30 years ago. What they overlooked was that many of France's regional train station platforms were built over 50 years before . . . when trains were a little narrower. The engineers assumed that the newer platforms were representative of all platforms when they weren't.

The Watson rule reminds you to check all the assumptions in your frame. It is a wink to Sherlock Holmes' sidekick. When the duo investigated a challenging mystery, Watson often failed to crack the case because he overlooked a critical clue. A good check that you've followed the Watson rule is to validate that you can justify all the claims in your frame.

	Without the rule	With the rule	
H+T	I work in NYC as the general manager of a startup.	I work in NYC as the general manager of a startup.	
	I want to go to London for a business trip.	I want to go to London for a business trip.	
D	However, I don't know **which plane to take.**	However, I don't know how I should go to London.	**Watson** Examine all your assumptions!
Q	How should I go from NYC to London for a business trip, given that i don't know **which plane to take?** ✗	How should I go from NYC to London for a business trip, given that I don't know how to go there? ✔	

Following the Watson rule might help you refocus your efforts. For instance, it might lead you to identify that some of the constraints that you thought you had to accommodate could in fact be relaxed (see below). In fact, checking your assumptions is so important that the entire next chapter is devoted to this topic.

Do we really need more sales agents?

Albrecht serves on the board of Agathon, a mid-sized Swiss manufacturing company. Agathon's high-tech grinding machines enable tool manufacturers to grind ultra-high-precision tools for turning and milling parts to a precision of a few micrometres. In addition, Agathon operates a business unit that produces guiding systems which are used, for instance, in moulding and punching tools. Here again, precision is critical to ensure that stamped sheet metal and moulded plastic pieces, like a Swatch wristband or med tech parts like syringes are produced to exact specifications. Because of its capabilities to produce the most exact guiding systems, Agathon is widely recognised as a global technology leader in this niche B2B market – a true hidden champion.

On the downside, Agathon has very limited market reach, a result of the high price of its products, especially compared to Asian competitors, and the set-up of its salesforce. For historical reasons, Agathon primarily operates through a small network of independent sales agents who sell both Agathon products and parts from other companies to die-and-mould builders, primarily in Europe.

During a strategy workshop, the top team and a group of more junior people explored how to increase sales for guiding systems throughout Europe, and particularly in Germany. The obvious quests that came to everyone's mind was how to increase the number of sales agents or how to ensure that they would spend more time promoting Agathon's products instead of other manufacturers' parts. The underlying assumption was that there was no other way to sell than through the sales agents, as it would be too costly to cover large sales areas and thousands of customers with an internal salesforce.

As the discussions progressed, however, one of the young talents offered to use a web-based sales platform as a way to inform customers about Agathon products. This idea, in turn, caused the team to broaden the quest. Instead of asking how to increase the number of sales agents or make each individual agent more productive, they now expanded it to 'how can we increase sales in Germany through different types of sales channels?' This in turn helped the team think differently about the overall framing of the challenge, which opened up a much broader solution space. Michael Merkel, CEO of Agathon, commented on this initiative: 'The fundamentally new strategic approach of involving a broad mix of skilled and motivated people from different areas and levels of the organisation transformed not only the quality of the strategy but also the commitment of the organisation toward the strategy.'

In summary, for Agathon, following the Watson rule resulted in removing some of the constraints that had underpinned their thinking, thereby uncovering new ways forward.

Checking your assumptions will help you develop a more robust frame, which should lead you to better solutions. Checking your assumptions will also enable you to better prepare for field questions from a sceptical audience.

Calibrate your level of confidence

Although an opinion voiced with a high level of confidence tends to carry more weight in a discussion, research shows that high confidence does not necessarily imply a higher probability of being correct.[10]

So what? Well, first you might want to validate that you are well calibrated. Tools such as those found at Clearerthinking.org[11] enable you to give a true/false answer to a random question (e.g., 'Melbourne, Australia had a larger metro population than Fuzhou, China in 2016') and a confidence level, from 50% ('guessing') to 99% ('incredibly confident'). Assessing your performance over a number of questions, you will be able to establish whether you tend to be underconfident, overconfident, or well calibrated.

In addition, you may want to keep in mind when hearing opinions from other people that they might not be particularly well calibrated.

//// USE YOUR FRAME TO IMPROVE YOUR THINKING (UP TO A POINT) ////

Your frame is a concise problem statement that you tailor to your audience. Someone familiar with your problem won't need as much context as someone who knows nothing about your hero, treasure, dragon, or quest. However, in all cases, your frame should be simple enough for your retired father or your teenage daughter to understand (see below).

A good frame is simple, clear . . . and brief[12]

Hero: Peugeot is a French car brand that is not presently selling in the US market.

Treasure: Peugeot aspires to enter the US market, which requires it to fulfil its distributions needs (defined as selling cars and servicing them during their lifetime).

Dragon: However, Peugeot does not have a distribution network in the US.

Quest: How should Peugeot fulfil its distribution needs in the US (defined as selling cars and servicing them during their lifetime), given that it does not have a distribution network?

If you think that your problem is too complex to be summarised in such a way, think again. After helping people with hundreds of frames, we have yet to come across a problem in any field – from corporate finance, to architecture, philosophy, or quantum physics – that cannot be summarised in a Hero-Treasure-Dragon-Quest sequence simple enough for an average teenager to understand. Synthesising the problem in such a way isn't necessarily easy, in fact, we can almost guarantee that it will be challenging, but it's always possible. And it's powerful, because summarising your problem in a clear sequence requires you to clarify your own thinking. With a simple, clear, and brief problem statement, you remove any ambiguity behind which you could hide, which makes you more accountable.

To illustrate, the box below features an example whose hero needs more than one phrase. However, even in this case that requires more context, the entire frame barely reaches half a page, which is the upper limit of what is needed for the overwhelming majority of problems.

We need a doctor![13]

Hero: In the US, before performing surgery on a patient, a doctor first requests the patient's insurance provider to approve the cost of surgery. To do so, the insurance company asks a board-certified physician ("expert") to decide whether the surgery is necessary (make a "go/no-go decision"). Instead of hiring experts, which is expensive, insurance companies often obtain their go/no-go decisions from third parties.

Sandra is the CEO of RWH, a start-up that provides go/no-go decisions that it obtains from partner medical schools where the experts are the schools' professors. RWH's service is in such high demand that Sandra's main challenge is to deliver enough go/no-go decisions to insurance companies. To do so, RWH recently signed an agreement with Major Medical School (MMS).

Treasure: Sandra wants RWH to continue delivering sufficient go/no-go decisions to insurance companies.

Dragon: However, MMS will not provide the go/no-go decisions that it had promised RWH.

Quest: How should RWH continue delivering sufficient go/no-go decisions to insurance companies, given that MMS will not provide the decisions that it had promised RWH?

In our experience, following two simple principles pays huge dividends when reworking a frame: (1) committing your thinking to paper and (2) not aiming for perfection.

Commit your thinking to paper

Novelist Flannery O'Connor said, 'I don't know what I think until I read what I say.' Writing down your thinking helps improve it in three ways. First, it creates a 'hard drive' where you can store information, which frees up your working memory – your ability to keep information in short-term memory and manipulate it. This is important because limits in working memory constrain our ability to solve problems.[14]

Second, writing down your thinking helps create a shared understanding among the team, a cornerstone of effective problem solving.[15]

Finally, it also helps you document your thinking as of today so that if you revise the scope of the project later on, that change will be the result of a conscious decision rather than unconscious scope creep.

Don't aim for perfection

A final word of caution: Don't get stuck trying to get the *right* frame or, even worse, the *perfect* one. First, because there's no such thing.[16] The maths problems that we all saw in school had one right answer and an infinity of wrong ones. Complex problems, however, are subjective (a consequence of being ill defined) and therefore don't have one objectively correct solution. Second, your frame should represent the understanding that you share with your stakeholders, but you're still early in the process. Chances are that as you progress, you will uncover new evidence that will make you update your frame. That's perfectly fine! Make your frame as good as you can make it for now, embrace that it's imperfect, and move forward.

The checklist below summarises the ideas that we covered in this chapter and the previous one. To help you internalise these ideas, we strongly encourage you to apply them on your project, which you can easily do in the Dragon Master™ app.

Frame checklist		
Substance: Hero-Treasure-Dragon-Quest	**Substance: Rules**	**Engagement & logistics**
• Generate various *quests* with appropriate type, scope, and phrasing • Choose the *quest* you prefer and articulate why • In the *hero*, include as much information as needed and as little as possible to specify the part of the universe of interest • In the *treasure*, specify the hero's aspiration • Make the *dragon* the one problem separating the hero from the treasure. Start it with 'however' • Make the *quest* the over-arching question that your project answers • Make the *quest* of the form: '**How should [the hero] get [the treasure], given [the dragon]?**'	• Follow *backpack*: Leave out any superfluous info. Carry the rest • Follow *rabbit*: Include necessary info *before* the quest • Follow *Dolly*: Always refer to things in the same way • Follow *Watson*: Check your assumptions • Make the frame understandable by a novice in just one read	• Engage all relevant stakeholders • Make the frame reflect the group's shared understanding • Clarify the project's logistics (time, money, others)

/////// CHAPTER TAKEAWAYS ///////

You can significantly improve your frame by making it simple and concise. Four rules can be useful handrails to develop a stronger frame:

1. **The Backpack rule:** Although a Tube map might be less accurate than a photo, it might be more useful. In your frame, include only the information that needs to be there.

2. **The Rabbit rule:** Chekhov's gun can only go off if you first introduced it: Don't present new information in the quest, it's too late.

3. **The Dolly rule:** Favour clarity over variety: Use language consistently – no synonyms or confusing pronouns.

4. **The Watson rule:** Don't build trains that won't fit the stations: Check your assumptions. You should be able to defend all the claims you make in your Hero-Treasure-Dragon-Quest sequence.

Keep it simple. Remember, in the end, your frame should be understandable by an average teenager – or a very smart dog. If your retired mother or teenage son cannot explain the frame back to you, it's not yet simple enough.

Write down your frame – both for your own sake and your team's.

Don't shoot for perfection. Do what you can, run it by others, use their feedback to improve your frame, and move forward. New evidence will surface, so you will need to update your frame anyway.

////////// CHAPTER 2 NOTES //////////

1 See discussion on p. 189 of Haran, U., I. Ritov and B. A. Mellers (2013). 'The role of actively open-minded thinking in information acquisition, accuracy, and calibration'. For a review, see pp. 157–161 of Arkes, H. R. and J. Kajdasz (2011). Intuitive theories of behavior. *Intelligence analysis: Behavioral and social scientific foundations*. B. Fischhoff and C. Chauvin, The National Academies Press**:** 143–168.

2 Adams, G. S., B. A. Converse, A. H. Hales and L. E. Klotz (2021). 'People systematically overlook subtractive changes.' *Nature* **592**(7853): 258–261.

3 Thompson, D. V., R. W. Hamilton and R. T. Rust (2005). 'Feature fatigue: When product capabilities become too much of a good thing.' *Journal of Marketing Research* **42**(4): 431–442.

4 See Cartwright, W. (2012). *Beck's representation of London's underground system: Map or diagram?* GSR. Jenny, B. (2006). 'Geometric distortion of schematic network maps.' *Bulletin of the Society of Cartographers* **40**(1): 15–18.

5 Rumelt on absorbing complexity. See p. 111 of Rumelt, R. P. (2011). *Good strategy/bad strategy: The difference and why it matters*, Rumelt, R. P. (2012).

6 Note the adjective 'meaningful' in the sentence. It is fine to include some non-meaningful information, let's call it *contextual* information, to help the audience get situated. That contextual information doesn't need to appear again elsewhere in the sequence . . . but you should include as little of such contextual information as possible.

7 See Higdon, M. J. (2009). 'Something judicious this way comes … The use of foreshadowing as a persuasive device in judicial narrative.' *University of Richmond Law Review* **44**: 1213.

8 See Rider, Y. and N. Thomason (2010). Cognitive and pedagogical benefits of argument mapping: LAMP guides the way to better thinking. *Knowledge cartography: Software tools and mapping techniques*. A. Okada, S. J. Buckingham Shum and T. Sherborne. London, Springer: 113–130; Twardy, C. (2010). 'Argument maps improve critical thinking.' *Teaching Philosophy* **27**(2): 95–116.

9 BBC News. (2014). 'French red faces over trains that are "too wide".' Retrieved March 14, 2021, from https://www.bbc.com/news/world-europe-27497727. Carnegy, H. (2014). New French trains too big for stations. *Financial Times*.

10 See, for instance, pp. 147–151 of Arkes, H. R. and J. Kajdasz (2011). Intuitive theories of behavior. *Intelligence analysis: Behavioral and social scientific foundations*. B. Fischhoff and C. Chauvin, The National Academies Press: 143–168. Bang, D., L. Aitchison, R. Moran, S. H. Castanon, B. Rafiee, A. Mahmoodi, J. Y. Lau, P. E. Latham, B. Bahrami and C. Summerfield (2017). 'Confidence matching in group decision-making.' *Nature Human Behaviour* **1**(6): 1–7.

11 Clearer Thinking. (2021). 'Make better decisions.' Retrieved 30 July, 2021, from https://www.clearerthinking.org.

12 See Kitman, J. L. (2018). Peugeot returns to U.S. to help people get around, but not with its cars. *New York Times*. Achment, O., L. Girard, S. Kanabar, N. Köhler, S. Schnorf and A. Chevallier (2020). Conquering America: Can Peugeot stage a successful return to the US? *IMD Case 7-2221*.

13 See Chevallier, A. (2019). 'A rock and a hard place at RWH.' *Case IMD-7-2186*.

14 Working memory constraining thinking. See Baddeley, A. (1992). 'Working memory.' *Science* **255**(5044): 556–559; Dufresne, R. J., W. J. Gerace, P. T. Hardiman and J. P. Mestre (1992). 'Constraining novices to perform expertlike problem analyses: Effects on schema acquisition.' *The Journal of the Learning Sciences* **2**(3): 307–331. See also Dunbar, K. N. and D. Klahr (2012). Scientific thinking and reasoning. *The Oxford handbook of thinking and reasoning*. K. J. Holyoak and R. G. Morrison. New York, Oxford University Press: 701–718.

15 Creating a shared understanding of the problem is an important milestone. See p. 83 of Riel, J. and R. L. Martin (2017). *Creating great choices: A leader's guide to integrative thinking*, Harvard Business Press. For the value of shared understanding, see, for instance, Porck, J. P., D. van Knippenberg, M. Tarakci, N. Y. Ateş, P. J. Groenen and M. de Haas (2020). 'Do group and organizational identification help or hurt intergroup strategic consensus?' *Journal of Management* **46**(2): 234–260;

and Lee, M. T. and R. L. Raschke (2020). 'Innovative sustainability and stakeholders' shared understanding: The secret sauce to "performance with a purpose".' *Journal of Business Research* **108**: 20–28.

16 See, for instance, pp. 266–267 of French, S., J. Maule and N. Papamichail (2009). *Decision behaviour, analysis and support*, Cambridge University Press. See also p. 280 of Hayes, J. R. (1989). *The complete problem solver.* New York, Routledge.

Chapter Three

Diagnose your problem

Chapters 1 and 2 showed how to summarise a complex problem in a Hero-Treasure-Dragon-Quest (HTDQ) sequence. As part of the process, the Watson rule advised you to check all assumptions in your HTDQ sequence. Following Watson is usually non-trivial, as it often requires uncovering the root causes of your problem – or diagnosing it. Let's look at how to do that.

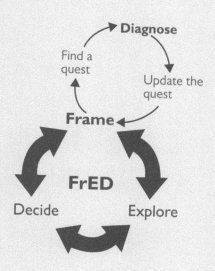

Misdiagnosing engine troubles on BD 092[1]

On 8 January, 1989, BD 092 – a Boeing 737-400 operated by British Midland – was en route from London Heathrow to Belfast International. While the plane was at 28,000 ft climbing to its cruise altitude, the flight crew suddenly sensed a strong vibration. Fumes and a burnt smell led them to think that one of the engines was malfunctioning. When the crew throttled back the right engine, the vibration stopped, so they thought that the right engine was the problem, and they turned it off.

However, the loss of vibration was coincidental; in reality, the left engine was the malfunctioning one. In the ensuing activity, as the crew attempted to reach a diversion airport, they did not validate their diagnosis. The left engine eventually failed completely during their final approach, and the plane crashed with neither engine running five hundred metres short of the runway. The accident killed 47 of the 126 people onboard.

Misdiagnosing engine troubles on BD 092 resulted in the crew framing the problem poorly, leading them to ask the question 'how do we manage our malfunctioning right engine?' when the left engine was the malfunctioning one. As it happens, poor framing is also common in the corporate world: In a two-year study we conducted at IMD, over 55% of executives we polled reported observing poor framing during strategic decisions in their organisation.[2]

So, we shouldn't feel that problem framing is a foolish expense of time separating us from getting things done, but rather an investment that is helping us build a robust foundation for the rest of our problem-solving efforts. In addition to the framing techniques you have acquired in Chapters 1 and 2, conducting a good diagnosis can help you frame effectively.

Now, you might ask why we propose to frame before diagnosing. Well, to start looking for the root causes of a problem, you need to have a sense of where to look. Otherwise, you risk 'boiling the ocean', that is, looking at everything imaginable but without having the time to analyse anything in detail. To be sure, diagnosing will probably lead you to adjust or even completely change your initial framing, and that is completely fine, as long as you have planned enough time to do so. However, the initial frame, consisting of a hero, a treasure, a dragon and a quest, will provide you with a first sense of where to direct your diagnostic efforts.

You can diagnose your problem using a two-step approach: First, identify the potential root causes, which you can do by using a *why* map – a visual breakdown of the problem's potential root causes. Second, identify which of these potential root causes are actually at play.

DRAW EFFECTIVE *WHY* ////// MAPS BY FOLLOWING THE ////// FOUR MAP RULES

Let's first consider how to identify potential root causes. Imagine that you have just been appointed the general director of a company, and you discover that it is not profitable. Why might this be the case? Maybe you are failing to attract enough new clients? Or perhaps your raw material costs are too high? Or maybe another factor is at play. Ultimately, making your company more profitable depends to a large extent on your ability to identify the underlying root cause (or root *causes* as there might be more than one). Just like the British Midland pilots who turned off the wrong engine, if you focus on reducing your raw material costs when what is really driving down your profits is that you don't have enough revenues from new clients, chances are that your measures won't be very effective.

Steal a page from the design thinking book[3]

Doug Dietz, an engineer at GE, designed large medical imaging equipment. A few years ago, Doug was in a hospital inspecting one of his MRI machines when he saw a little girl terrified by the prospect of being put into the loud, cold machine. This wasn't an isolated instance: Children were so scared by MRI machines that 80% had to be sedated before they could be scanned. Following a design-thinking approach, Doug immersed himself into the world of these little patients to find out how they thought so that he could improve their experience. These methods included:

- **Observe** – Watch and listen to users in the setting in which they encounter the problem and experience the artifacts they use to solve it.

- **Engage** – Talk with users and capture how they say they behave, think, and feel.

- **Immerse** – Go through the experience himself.

Doug used the insights from his analysis to develop a very different type of solution than he might have had if he had only used an analytical process: He turned the high-tech MRI into a colourful pirate ship, produced sound effects, and handed out costumes. He also created a story in which the MRI machine was a pirate ship, and the patient had to be very quiet and still to evade the pirates! Exams became immersive adventures where kids forgot about their fears and embraced the experience.

The changes were so successful that kids who had gone through the MRI asked if they could do it again. There were also positive business implications to the changes, as the number of repeat exams plummeted, all with almost no need for sedation. Happy customers. Faster processes. All told, an inspiring story of design and change.

Diagnosing the root causes of the problem (understanding what created a poor experience) rather than addressing the perceived problem (forcing kids to comply with the process in place) helped Doug identify a great solution.

The complex problems you face have lots of potential root causes, so considering them all is usually challenging. In addition, some are causes of others, which makes untangling them difficult.

Just as a map can be invaluable when navigating an unfamiliar territory, mapping out the potential root causes of your problem can also be immensely useful. That's where drawing a *why* map comes in.

Let's walk through a *why* map. Imagine that your company isn't profitable. Why could that be? Well, low profitability might originate from two reasons. Either your revenues are too low or your costs are too high (or both, yes, but that's already accounted for in these two so let's not repeat it). Pushing your analysis, you might hypothesise that your revenues are too low because your revenues from new clients are too low or your revenues from returning clients are too low. Similarly on the cost side, high costs might result from high fixed costs or high variable costs, and the latter might be driven up by high raw materials costs or high effort costs. You get the idea.

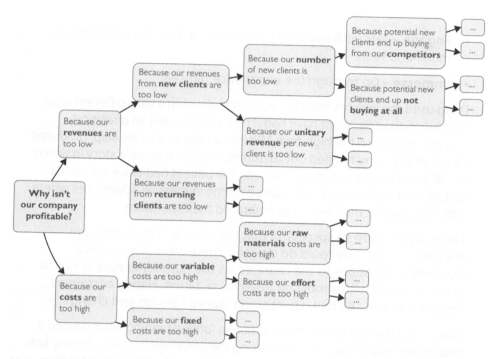

Using this mapping technique, you can identify all the potential root causes for your problem by moving in two dimensions: vertically, you explore new kinds of root causes; horizontally, you get into more details. Mapping is an effective way to actively structure the universe of potential root causes of a problem. So it's worth learning how to develop *why* maps. Effective *why* maps follow four rules. Let's look at them.

Mapping rule 1: *Why* maps answer a single *why* question

To kick off the diagnosis, choose which aspect of your frame you'd benefit most from looking into. In principle, you can concentrate on any aspect of the quest with a *why* question: 'Why this hero?', 'Why this treasure?' or 'Why this dragon?' All of these questions might be interesting and relevant. However, we have found that it is usually most beneficial to focus on either the treasure or the dragon. For instance, you may question why a specific treasure is important to you, or why you failed to get it in previous attempts.

Similarly, you may want to better understand your dragon by asking why your dragon is a problem, or why you haven't already overcome your dragon.

In an ideal world, you would have the resources to ask several of these *why* questions . . . or perhaps even all! In practice, however, your resources are limited, so you will often only be able to ask one. Therefore, your challenge is to identify which *why* question would bring you the most. As with choosing your quest, engage your core stakeholders to help you generate several candidates, compare them, and select the best one.

Once you've chosen your *why* question, start drawing your map. Good maps are clear, so clear in fact that they look simple. But as with Hero-Treasure-Dragon-Quest sequences, achieving that simplicity is usually challenging.

Mapping rule 2: *Why* maps go from the question to potential root causes

Within a map, you move by asking two types of questions. Horizontally, asking *why?* helps you get into more detailed potential root causes. Vertically, asking *what else?* helps you uncover new kinds of potential root causes.

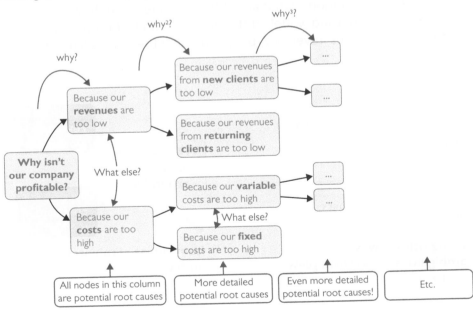

Toyota's Total Quality Management approach advises that you uncover the root causes of the problem by asking *why* five times.[4] That's a good general rule, but you might benefit from asking *why* more times for some branches and fewer times for others. More than the number of levels, what matters is that you develop the map sufficiently so that its items, the so-called *nodes*, are no longer conceptual (e.g. 'because our raw materials costs are too high') but concrete (e.g. 'because we use 10% more carbon fibre in our products than is needed'). That is, you should use however many levels of *whys* it takes to get to a point where a reasonably knowledgeable person won't ask: 'So, what does this mean more specifically?' Note that you might not need to develop all branches to the same level – some might be sufficiently explicit after just a couple of levels while others might need many more. This disparity is perfectly fine.[5]

In your *why* map, follow simple guidelines to make your thinking clear and concise:

- **Use full declarative sentences**.[6] Phrase each node as a full declarative sentence that answers the question. That is, make each node an idea, not just a title. That will help you and others avoid ambiguities. Consider for instance a map that answers 'why isn't our company profitable?' with a node that simply states a title, say, 'revenues'. That node is ambiguous: what about the revenues? Are they overly diversified, decreasing, widely differing across units, or too small? If the node just states 'revenues', people reading the map will need to

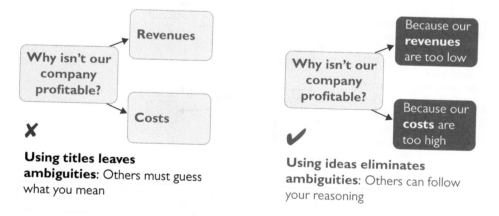

Using titles leaves ambiguities: Others must guess what you mean

Using ideas eliminates ambiguities: Others can follow your reasoning interpret it, which will yield differing interpretations. Conversely, by making each node an idea – 'because our revenues are too low' – you remove the ambiguities. People might still disagree with your logic, and that might trigger a debate, which is great, but at least your thinking is understandable.

- **Phrase nodes in a clear, consistent manner.** Aside from using declarative sentences, you can dramatically increase the quality of your *why* maps by phrasing nodes clearly and consistently. First, start each node with 'because'. This is only fair, since you're answering a *why* question. Also, use a parallel phrase structure within a given group of nodes and highlight the elements that are changing.

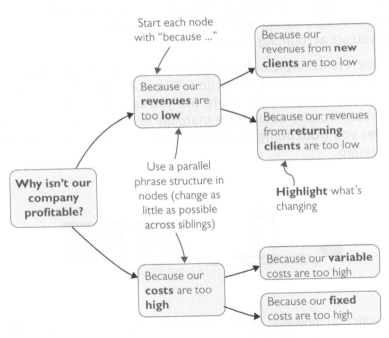

You might be tempted to ignore this recommendation. After all, the fewer the words, the better, so omitting 'because' should help. But after coaching hundreds of people on drawing maps, we find that those who structure their nodes following these guidelines consistently show better logic. We think that this is because forcing us to abide by this structure forces us to clean up our thinking.

- **Synthesise your map in formal root causes**. Developing a *why* map often results in dozens of nodes, making it impractical to analyse each independently. Instead, it makes more sense to cluster them into judicious formal root causes. To keep things practical, aim for two to five such root causes.

Mapping rule 3: *Why* maps are MECE

One key success factor of effective *why* maps is their MECEness. MECE (pronounced 'me-see') stands for *mutually exclusive and collectively exhaustive*. MECE thinking refers to the process of organising a set of items so that you are accounting for each exactly once.[7]

For a concrete example of how MECE thinking works, imagine that while driving you get to a t-junction. What can you do? Well, you may continue straight or turn left, but you can't do both at the same time. These two alternatives are *mutually exclusive*; that is, doing one precludes you from doing the other. In other words, the alternatives don't overlap.

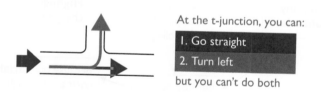

At the t-junction, you can:

| 1. Go straight |
| 2. Turn left |

but you can't do both

At the t-junction, however, going straight and turning left aren't your only two alternatives. You may also reverse, stop, change direction, or do a few more things.

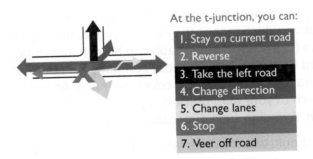

At the t-junction, you can:

1. Stay on current road
2. Reverse
3. Take the left road
4. Change direction
5. Change lanes
6. Stop
7. Veer off road

If you list all potential alternatives, then the list is *collectively exhaustive*. There are no gaps in the list of alternatives.

A MECE list, then, has no overlaps (ME) and no gaps (CE). Being collectively exhaustive, you don't forget any alternative, so you're thoroughly creative. Being mutually exclusive, you force yourself to understand how the alternatives relate to one another, so you're clearer in your thinking.

MECEness is a simple concept. Making your thinking MECE, however, usually isn't trivial. If you are lucky, your problem breaks down into clean-enough parts, such as what to do at a t-junction. However, if your problem involves more nebulous concepts – developing a business model, getting people motivated, reshaping an organisation's culture – making your thinking MECE can be challenging.

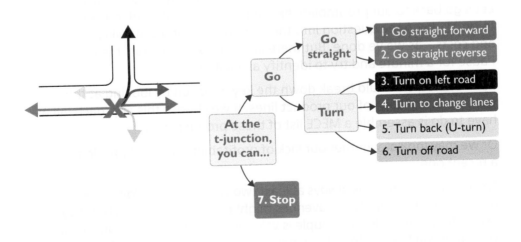

To summarise, good maps have a MECE structure. Their branches are *mutually exclusive*, which means they don't overlap. In the profitability example above (see p. 81), if your map's top branch investigates how low revenues might be the reason why your company isn't profitable, then your bottom branch should not also cover revenues. Addressing revenues in the top branch of your map precludes you from also addressing it in the bottom branch. Avoiding such duplications, you keep things clear.

The branches should also be *collectively exhaustive*, leaving no gaps. Since profitability equals revenues minus costs, addressing revenues and costs is sufficient, and your map shouldn't address other themes.

So far, we have talked about what MECE thinking is, but we haven't given you concrete ideas on how to make your thinking MECE. We'll do that in the next chapter, but here's one idea: To help you be CE, don't judge your ideas. Include all the potential root causes of your problem in your *why* map, no matter how improbable they are. This is because you don't know what you don't know. Include all the logically valid answers to your *why* question, no matter how seemingly outlandish they are. Don't auto-limit yourself; ideate now, you'll evaluate later.[8]

Mapping rule 4: *Why* maps are insightful[9]

A good *why* map has a structure that is both logically valid *and* useful. Let's go back to our profitability example. On the first level, one avenue is to break down the question into the components of profitability – revenues and costs – as we've done. But there are other ways to start the map. Pause for a minute and try to identify at least one.

For instance, we could break down the key question by looking at the profitability of each of our product lines. If we choose this approach, all we have to do is assemble a MECE list of these product lines.

Or we may look at whether our lack of profitability is an old problem versus a recent one.

The point is that there is always at least two ways to break down a question or a node in the map. These avenues might not be easy to find, but they exist. Identifying at least a couple is valuable because it helps you look at your question from different perspectives, which might trigger fresh insights.

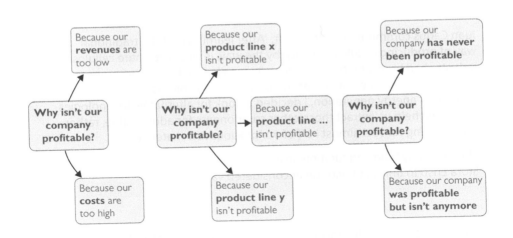

Stora Enso rethinks how it thinks about trees

Stora Enso is a Finnish-Swedish global provider of renewable solutions in packaging, biomaterials, wooden construction, and paper (the hero). During the mid 2000s, paper demand – one of Stora Enso's main revenue drivers at the time – declined rapidly. This triggered the company to look for new usage possibilities for their trees in the early 2010s (the treasure).

However, they didn't know how to do so (the dragon), probably because the mindset in the senior management team remained on traditional applications of tree components. Jouko Karvinen, Stora Enso's CEO at the time, observed: 'We were only thinking in terms of the physical elements of the tree: the long planks inside that could be used for construction, the small parts that were turned into pulp for paper production and for making heating pellets, and the waste products, such as the bark, that were used right away to create energy.' Their breakdown was MECE: it included all the important elements of a physical tree (CE) and there were no overlaps (ME). However, this way of 'cutting the tree' failed to generate innovative usage ideas – it lacked insightfulness.

In response, Stora Enso hired an industry outsider – Juan Carlos Bueno, an industrial engineer – who looked at trees from a different perspective. Instead of decomposing a tree into its physical elements, he decomposed it in a MECE set of biochemical elements. The pieces that appeared then were quite different, including lignin, cellulose and hemicellulose, which opened up a whole new range of business opportunities. One of those is TreeToTextile AB, a joint venture with H&M and IKEA to develop new textile fibres using tree cellulose.

Juan Carlos commented on this shift: 'After learning that the traditional way of producing cellulose – which by the way, is what the entire cellulose industry had been practising for decades – called for the exclusive separation of cellulose while the remainder components of the biomass were burnt as biofuel for energy generation, I decided to look for alternative technologies that could help us extract those other components for added value, rather than burning for fuel almost half of our precious raw material.'

The takeaway? Looking for more insightfulness in how they 'cut' a tree led Stora Enso to unlock previously unconsidered value.

In the end, you can only start your map with one of the structures you consider. So, which should you use? Well, the most insightful one of course! In the profitability example above, given that all three candidate structures are logically valid, insightfulness comes down to usefulness, and which of these structures is most useful depends on your circumstances. If, for instance, your profitability varies greatly across product lines, it might be most insightful to use the second candidate structure, as it will help you tackle the lines that are problematic and leave alone the ones that work well. Similarly, if your lack of profitability is a recent issue, using that third candidate structure might help you ask that all-important 'what changed?' question. With this in mind, you may want to start drawing your own *why* map.

////// CONDUCT YOUR ANALYSIS //////

All we've done by drawing a *why* map is lay out the potential root causes of our problem. Sticking with our scientific approach and the probabilistic mindset it entails, each of these is nothing more than a hypothesis that needs to be tested.

Next, we need to investigate whether evidence supports or opposes these hypotheses, which you can do with the four-step LEAD approach:[10]

1 **Locate the evidence**. Identify and gather the types of evidence relevant to the hypothesis.

2 **Evaluate the evidence**. Assess the quality of the piece of evidence.

3 **Synthesise the evidence**. Assess the body of evidence as a whole, understanding its 'so what?'.

4 **Decide**. Identify whether you can accept or reject the hypothesis or whether more information is needed.

One important consideration: *favour opposing evidence.* For instance, let's assume that we want to test the root cause: 'our company isn't profitable because our revenues from new clients are too low.' Relevant evidence will affect the likelihood of the hypothesis, increasing it (for supporting evidence) or decreasing it (for opposing evidence). But beware, as focusing on supporting evidence can promote overconfidence.[11]

Note that running a rigorous analysis helps you develop robust insights, which will increase the likelihood of finding a more impactful solution. But that rigor will also probably improve your engagement with your key stakeholders as you will be able to show that you were thorough and impartial in collecting and assessing evidence.

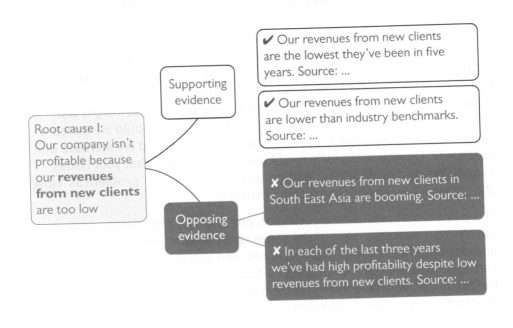

For each hypothesis, you will probably find both supporting *and* opposing evidence.[12] It is a fact of life (although not a pleasing one!) that evidence is usually incomplete, inconclusive, and ambiguous. Furthermore, our biases push us to look for evidence that supports our views, which can lead to all sorts of troubles. Therefore, we are better served looking for opposing evidence. To this end, identify what evidence would change your mind and try to get that evidence. Your job is to seek the highest quality evidence that you can find – focusing your efforts on finding *opposing* evidence – to, in the end, decide whether you ought to reject that the hypothesis you're testing is indeed a root cause or accept it.[13]

At last, keep in mind that establishing that a hypothesis is indeed a root cause does not exonerate other hypotheses. Sometimes, our profitability is low because our revenues are low *and* our costs are high.[14]

//////// UPDATE YOUR QUEST – REFRAME THE PROBLEM ////////

Uncovering your problem's root causes helps you understand your problem better. For instance, your diagnosis might lead you to conclude that your company is not profitable because your revenues are low. Updating your Hero-Treasure-Dragon-Quest sequence to incorporate that insight will make it more specific: Instead of asking a broad 'How should we increase our profitability?' question, you can now ask 'How should we increase our revenues?' Or your diagnostic might lead you to realise that your issues expand beyond profitability, leading you to reframe your problem as 'How should we increase our return on investment?'

The point is that return on investment, profitability, and revenues are interrelated concepts, part of the same set of Russian dolls. Which one you address depends on your circumstances, and you won't know until you consider different parts of that set of dolls. Diagnosing helps you choose the focus that will have the highest return; that is, where investing one unit of effort will generate the largest dividends.

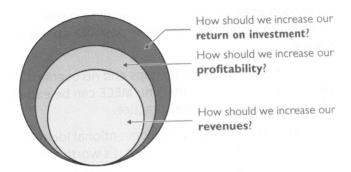

How should we increase our **return on investment?**

How should we increase our **profitability?**

How should we increase our **revenues?**

We strongly encourage you to put these ideas into practice by drawing your own *why* map (here, too, the Dragon Master™ app can help). Once you've run your diagnostic analysis, modify your HTDQ sequence to reflect what you've just learned.

Summarising, all that we have done in Chapters 1, 2 and 3 was in the name of developing as good a quest as we could. Next, we'll switch gears and explore alternatives – that is, potential answers to this quest.

///////// CHAPTER TAKEAWAYS /////////

Addressing a symptom instead of the underlying disease can result in an ineffective effort, so you should diagnose your problem. As a general rule, assume that what you think the problem is when you first encounter it isn't the problem that you should solve.

Drawing a *why* map can help you identify your problem's potential root causes. Effective *why* maps obey four rules:

- Mapping rule 1: They answer a single *why* question.
- Mapping rule 2: They go from the question to potential root causes.
- Mapping rule 3: They use a MECE structure.
- Mapping rule 4: They are insightful.

Evaluate the likelihood of each root cause by analysing relevant evidence, striving to obtain as high-quality evidence as possible – particularly opposing evidence.

Thinking MECE means that you leave no gaps and no overlaps in your thinking. Be prepared: making your thinking MECE can be extremely challenging! Becoming good at it takes practice.

Being CE will require you to think beyond conventional ideas. Some of these creative ideas will feel odd or dumb, but it's worth considering them, because you don't know what good ideas they can spark, so don't auto censor.

In the end, conclude on your problem's root causes and synthesise your analysis by updating your frame.

/////////// CHAPTER 3 NOTES ///////////

1 Air Accidents Investigations Branch (1990). Report on the accident to Boeing 737-400 G-OBME near Kegworth, Leicestershire on 8 January, 1989 (Aircraft Accident Report 4/90). HMSO. London.

2 A majority of executives who come to IMD . . . . During a two-year study at IMD, we asked over 450 senior managers and executives to share the prevalent issues that they observed in their organisations during problem solving and 55% of the respondents reported framing issues. These results were consistent across geographies, industries, and seniority levels.

3 See pp. 16–24 of Kelley, T. and D. Kelley (2013). *Creative confidence: Unleashing the creative potential within us all*, Currency.

4 See, for instance, Arnheiter, E. D. and J. Maleyeff (2005). 'The integration of lean management and Six Sigma.' *The TQM Magazine* **17**(1): 5–18. Chapter 7 of Andersen, B. and T. Fagerhaug (2006). *Root cause analysis: Simplified tools and techniques*. Milwaukee, WI, ASQ Quality Press. Card,

A. J. (2017). 'The problem with "5 whys".' *BMJ Quality & Safety* **26**(8): 671–677. Chiarini, A., C. Baccarani and V. Mascherpa (2018). 'Lean production, Toyota production system and kaizen philosophy.' *The TQM Journal.*

5 For a discussion of when to stop going into more details, see pp. 65–67 and 123–124 of Chevallier, A. (2016). *Strategic thinking in complex problem solving.* Oxford, UK, Oxford University Press.

6 This approach parallels using an assertion-evidence structure for designing slides, which has been shown to enhance understanding and recollection. See Garner, J. K. and M. P. Alley (2016). 'Slide structure can influence the presenter's understanding of the presentation's content.' *International Journal of Engineering Education* **32**(1): 39–54; and Garner, J. and M. Alley (2013). 'How the design of presentation slides affects audience comprehension: A case for the assertion–evidence approach.' *International Journal of Engineering Education* **29**(6): 1564–1579.

7 MECE is old. Some consultants like to say MECE thinking is a McKinsey thing, but it's been around for a long time. It has been present in philosophy for centuries (initially formulated by John Duns Scotus in the thirteenth century) and it's an essential part of probability theory.

8 See, for instance, Basadur, M. (1995). 'Optimal ideation-evaluation ratios.' *Creativity Research Journal* **8**(1): 63–75.

9 Maps are popular. Our question maps – the *why* map of this chapter and the *how* maps of the next – are just one of many visual tools to solve complex problems. For a review, see p. 47 of Chevallier (2016).

10 Adapted from pp. 89–92 of Sim, L. J., L. Parker and S. K. Kumanyika (2010). *Bridging the evidence gap in obesity prevention: A framework to inform decision making.* Washington, DC, The National Academies Press. (And, yes, the adaptation means that the LEAD acronym no longer works but we kept it because LESD is slightly less catchy.) Working with evidence can be tricky. Working with evidence can rapidly get technical. So, for a start, follow the four-step process outlined in this chapter. If you're interested in more, see Tecuci, G., D. A. Schum, D. Marcu and M. Boicu (2014). 'Computational approach and cognitive assistant for evidence–based reasoning in intelligence analysis.' *International Journal of Intelligent Defence Support Systems* **5**(2): 146–172; and Tecuci, G.,

D. Schum, M. Boicu, D. Marcu and K. Russell (2011). 'Toward a computational theory of evidence-based reasoning.' 18th International Conference on Control Systems and Computer Science, *University Politehnica of Bucharest*. For an in-depth treatment of how to work with evidence, see Anderson, T., D. Schum and W. Twining (2005). *Analysis of evidence.* New York, Cambridge University Press.

11 See Walters, D. J., P. M. Fernbach, C. R. Fox and S. A. Sloman (2017). 'Known unknowns: A critical determinant of confidence and calibration.' *Management Science* **63**(12): 4298–4307.

12 For a brief discussion of how to work with evidence, see pp. 97–102 of Chevallier, A. (2016). *Strategic thinking in complex problem solving.* Oxford, UK, Oxford University Press. For an in-depth treatment, see Anderson, T., D. Schum and W. Twining (2005). *Analysis of evidence.* New York, Cambridge University Press. Promoting evidence-based reasoning. The University of Melbourne's SWARM project strikes a sweet spot between structuring analysis and letting teams use their specific strengths to make predictions. See Van Gelder, T., R. De Rozario and R. O. Sinnott (2018). 'SWARM: Cultivating evidence-based reasoning.' *Computing in Science & Engineering* **20**(6): 22–34.

13 Formally, we cannot accept a hypothesis but only fail to reject it. However, here we'll just say 'accept' for simplicity sake.

14 In medicine, this condition is called *comorbidity.* See First, M. B. (2005). 'Mutually exclusive versus co-occurring diagnostic categories: The challenge of diagnostic comorbidity.' *Psychopathology* **38**(4): 206–210.

Part II
—

EXPLORE – Identify alternatives and criteria

Recall that you need four components to solve your problem:

- The overarching question that summarises your problem – the *quest*,
- Various *alternatives* to answer that question,
- *Criteria* that will help you identify which of these alternatives you prefer, and
- The *evaluations* of each alternative on each criterion.

Now that we have a quest, let's shift our focus to exploring alternatives and criteria.

Chapter 4 shows how you can explore the solution space using a close cousin of the *why* map: the *how* map. Chapter 5 will show how to explore criteria that you can use to choose the most promising alternative.

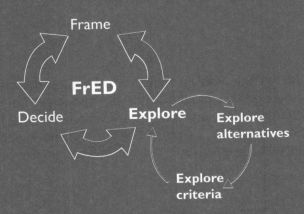

Chapter Four

Map the solution space – Explore alternatives

So far, we have framed the problem in the form of a quest that clearly specifies the hero, the treasure and the dragon. At this point, it can be immensely tempting to jump into pursuing the treasure using whichever solution that first occurs to us. But, often, the obvious solution isn't the best one, and letting our autopilot (our System 1 thinking) take the lead would result in a suboptimal approach.[1]

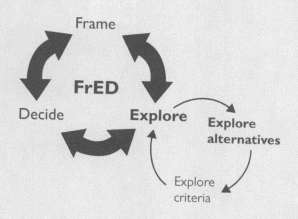

Consider the example of a global business services company with operations in Australia. The country manager wanted $20 million from headquarters to pursue a new business opportunity. When her proposal was turned down, her initial reaction was to resign. But her team persuaded her to explore other ways of pursuing the business opportunity, such as partnering with another organisation, which eventually proved successful. Stepping out to look beyond the obvious solutions can be valuable.[2]

This chapter shows how to avoid this common pitfall, providing a systematic approach to explore wide-ranging options that can be developed into concrete alternatives.[3]

The process is the same as the one we used for uncovering root causes.[4] First, we use divergent thinking to generate options, drawing a *how* map. Once we feel that we have exhausted our creativity, we use convergent thinking by summarising the potential options into a set of concrete alternatives that we feel have the greatest potential. We'll then compare the benefits and drawbacks of the alternatives in a systematic manner (see Chapter 6).

/// MOVE LEFT TO RIGHT BY APPLYING /// THE FOUR MAP RULES

Effective *how* maps obey the same four map rules as effective *why* maps with only minor changes owed to the different type of question asked. Let's review them.

Mapping rule 1: *How* maps answer a single *how* question

The *how* map answers a single question, typically of the form: 'How may [the hero] get [the treasure].' For instance, 'How may we increase our company's profitability, given that . . . ?' Notice the delicate phrasing of the question: 'How *may* we' or 'How *might* we' but not 'How should we'. This is to promote exploring ideas, even seemingly absurd ones, by delaying their evaluation to a later stage. We've stolen this approach from design thinkers, who deliberately choose their words to create space for maximum freedom of thinking.[5]

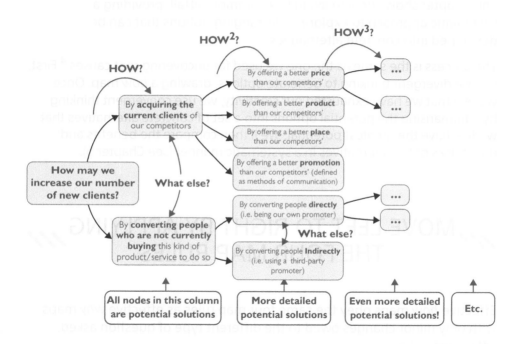

An important implication is that every single node in the map – the *options* – must answer the full question without the help of another node, that is, independently. To explain, let's look at an example. If you answer the question 'How may I go from NYC to London?' with 'By travelling by sea/air/ground', each of these options is independent: it answers the question without requiring the support from another option. You can think of them as channels.

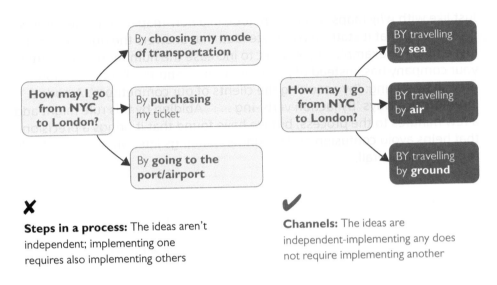

✘
Steps in a process: The ideas aren't independent; implementing one requires also implementing others

✔
Channels: The ideas are independent-implementing any does not require implementing another

In contrast, you might be tempted to answer the same question by listing what you would need to do to get from NYC to London; say, choosing a means of transportation, purchasing a ticket, and going to the airport. But those steps aren't independent: to get from NYC to London, you need to do each one of them. In other words, those aren't options but steps in a process. Successful *how* maps use channels, not steps in a process.

Mapping rule 2: *How* maps go from the question to alternatives

To draw your map, use two questions. Horizontally, ask *how*, typically three times or more. Vertically, create new branches by asking *what else?* This will lead you to chart out the solution space, identifying ever more precise (from left to right) and ever more creative (up and down) options. Continue asking 'how' until the options are concrete enough for you to envision how they could be implemented. For instance, one way how to get from NYC to London is to fly in an economy seat on BA 1511.

Just like with *why* maps, write each node in a *how* map as a full declarative sentence so that it states a complete idea that answers the question, not just a title. For example, if you want to increase the number of clients that your company has, instead of just saying 'competitors' clients', be more precise by stating: 'by acquiring the clients of our competitors'. A node's structure is always 'By [action verb]-ing . . . ' Abiding by this rule might add a few minutes to the process, but we have found that it brings a precision that helps avoid confusion and misunderstandings later on, so you're likely to save time overall.

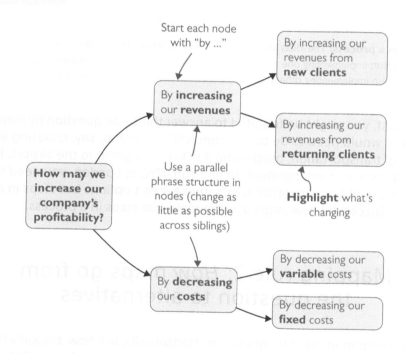

Mapping rule 3: *How* maps have a MECE structure

A *how* map has two key functions. The first is to help explore the solution space, to think of new ideas. The second is to systematically organise that space so that you consider all potential answers exactly once. And, yes, that means using a MECE structure.

In case you're questioning the necessity of actually mapping your solution space, consider this: By representing a physical space, a geographic map helps you choose your route to your destination. No one will argue the value of a map when placed in an unfamiliar location. Well, by helping you explore and organise alternatives, a *how* map fulfils the same function for the solution space, so that you can choose how to get to your treasure.

Making the structure of your map MECE can be challenging. To help you do so, follow the same approach as when developing your *why* map (see Chapter 3). In addition, using a few more ideas will help you for both types of maps:

- **Limit the sub-nodes under any given node to 3–5**: When a node has lots of sub-nodes, it becomes difficult to keep the structure MECE or validate MECEness. We can all remember being presented a slide with 15 bullet points that triggers us to immediately check out mentally (and turn to our smart phones) because it was impossible to make sense of the mess.

  Limiting the number of sub-nodes doesn't mean that you don't present concrete ideas! All it means is that instead of aggregating all your ideas on one level, you progress more gradually. At the same time, don't leave any node with a single sub-node, as this is indicative of a problem: Either your sub-node isn't CE (it needs at least one sibling) or the node and sub-node can be combined into a single node.

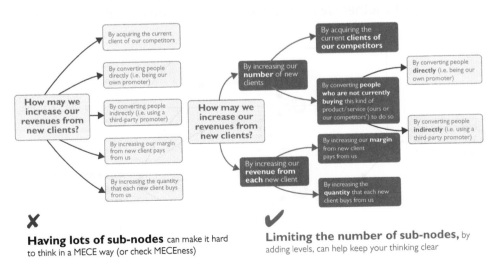

✗

Having lots of sub-nodes can make it hard to think in a MECE way (or check MECEness)

✔

Limiting the number of sub-nodes, by adding levels, can help keep your thinking clear

- **Use logic to promote ideation**: In our experience, using a map with a MECE structure can unleash your creativity by putting logic to work. For instance, if one of your nodes says 'by converting people who currently buy from our competitors to buy from us', you can use that node to identify other sources of new clients. If we can get new clients by 'stealing' them from our competitors, where else could we get new clients from? Maybe 'By converting people who are not currently buying this kind of product/service (ours or our competitors') to buy from us'. In this case, putting logic to work for you means that you'll be looking for all sources of new clients. Creating nodes, you set empty 'mental buckets' that prompt your mind with a directed stimulus to fill them up with ideas. In our experience, this prompted ideation is much more efficient and leads to a broader range of ideas than only working with a blank sheet.

  Now, don't fool yourself: Most ideas in the map will not be feasible or desirable, so you'll end up abandoning most, but don't let that stop you from thinking more innovatively. Remember, developing the map, you *generate* ideas. You'll *evaluate* them later.

- **Let the nodes be ICE (independent and collectively exhaustive)**: It is the structure of the map that is MECE. So if an idea is in one part of the map, that precludes it from being in another (the structure is ME) and the map encompasses all potential ideas (CE). However, the nodes in the map, the ideas, are independent and collectively exhaustive, or ICE. Here, 'independent' means that an idea can be pursued without the help of another idea in the map. So several ideas *might* be pursued

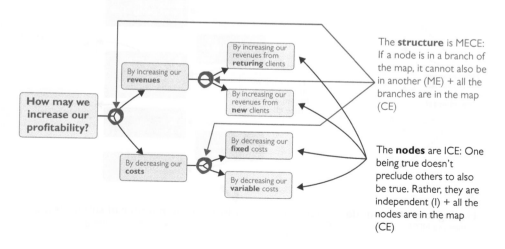

concomitantly, but no idea *needs* another one (see section '*how* maps answer a single *how* question', above).

Mapping rule 4: *How* maps are insightful

A good *how* map doesn't just contain lots of ideas in a MECE structure. It also helps you get to promising alternatives. That means that they need to be insightful: logically correct and adding value. Let's look at the travelling-from-NYC-to-London example again. You could start your map in a variety of ways, including highlighting the means of transportation:

- *Type*: say, 'by travelling by [ground/air/sea]'
- *Price*: say, 'by travelling using a [free/paying] means of transportation'
- *Carbon footprint*: 'by travelling using a means of transportation that has a [negative/neutral/positive] carbon footprint'
- *Riskiness*: 'by travelling using a means of transportation that has an associated [low/neutral/high] risk'

Or its *speed, convenience, comfort, flexibility, anonymity,* . . . . Indeed, there are numerous ways to start your map! So, how should you start your map? Well, using the most insightful, of course! But even within our definition of insightfulness (logically valid and useful; see Chapter 3), insightfulness means different things to different people.

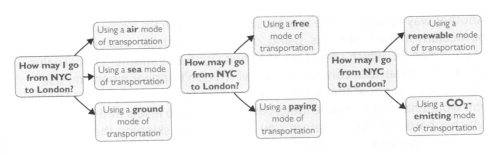

For instance, perhaps you are extremely environmentally conscious and, like Greta Thunberg who sailed across the Atlantic to go to a UN climate summit, you'll only consider renewable means of transportation.[6]

Here, the third structure might be most helpful to help you zero in on the avenues worth considering further. Or you might be like most business and tourism travellers, preferring more conventional approaches; then the first approach probably provides the most useful categorisation. Whatever the case, you won't know how insightful a first cut is until you compare it to another, so try to consider at least two first cuts, and then expand the map.

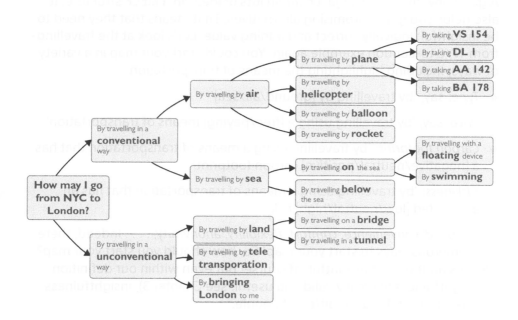

Another way to help you be more insightful is to refrain from using 'other', particularly in the first levels. Using 'other' automatically makes that level of your map CE, which seems great at first sight. But another critical value of a map is to surface concrete ideas, which don't appear when you use 'other'; at least not at that level of the map. To test your map's MECEness, you would have to integrate ideas coming from two levels of the map, which is harder to do. Therefore, you are better off skipping the use of 'other' for the sake of insightfulness.

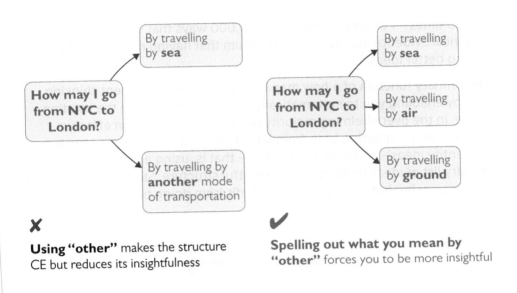

✗

Using "other" makes the structure
CE but reduces its insightfulness

✔

**Spelling out what you mean by
"other"** forces you to be more insightful

One exception to the don't-use-other guideline is when you want to create
a placeholder to return to later. Another exception is when you are already
at higher levels, so any part of the map only influences a limited portion of
the solution space.

MOVE RIGHT TO LEFT TO CREATE ADDITIONAL OPTIONS

Psychologist Alex Osborn, who popularised brainstorming, said that 'the
best way to have a good idea is to have many ideas'. Similarly, Nobel-
Prize laureate Linus Pauling pointed out that 'the way to get good ideas
is to get lots of ideas and throw the bad ones away'. For an illustration
of the approach in practice, consider Edison's famous experiments of
passing electricity through hundreds of materials for several years before
selecting carbon filaments. He is often quoted as saying, 'I have not failed

10,000 times – I've successfully found 10,000 ways that will not work'. Empirical evidence also supports this claim that having more ideas helps having better ideas.[7]

The primary function of a *how* map is to assist in this divergent-thinking task by enabling you to systematically explore and organise the solution space. In the overwhelming majority of cases, developing an effective map entails progressing both from left to right – that is, using a structure to identify ideas – *and* from right to left – that is, using an unstructured laundry list of ideas to identify an insightful structure. Start from whichever side you prefer, but you'll probably benefit from doing both during your analysis.

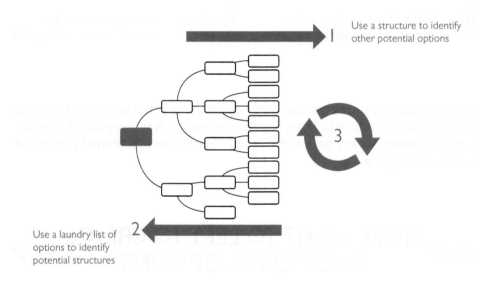

Use a structure to identify other potential options

Use a laundry list of options to identify potential structures

We have discussed the left-to-right way of developing *how* maps at length. Let's now take a brief look at three concrete ways to generate novel ideas: applying the solution of a similar problem, reframing your problem, or relaxing some of your pre-imposed constraints.

Promote (constructive!) dissent[8]

In some cultures, particularly in those with high Power Distance, groups can easily default to the HiPPO – the Highest Paid Person's Opinion – or other forms of undesirable consensus. Why should consensus be undesirable? Well, the self-censorship of lower-ranking group members prevents the team from benefiting from the friction of different perspectives to innovate.

A diverse group of stakeholders can help avoid group members thinking too much alike. Diversity includes *identity diversity*, which encompasses the age, gender, and cultural and ethnicity identity of the people; and *functional diversity*, which captures how people represent and solve problems.[9] Identity diversity can help reduce the harmful effect of correlated experiences while functional diversity might help bring about a more exhaustive search of the solution space.[10] Research has shown that the latter has positive impact on a team's performance.[11]

Overall, it is desirable to assemble a team with diverse perspectives and complementary expertise.[12] Vigorous debates ahead of the decision are useful and dissent can be an effective means to avoid groupthink (that is, group members becoming less independent[13]) or other suboptimal convergences of opinions.[14]

In addition, if you are the most senior person in the team, consider staying out of the idea-generation process altogether. Not because you won't have good ideas, but because your presence might limit the creativity of other team members.[15]

Various approaches exist to promote dissent, including *instructed dissent*, which consists of asking a subset of the team to adopt a position opposite to the consensus (playing devil's advocate) regardless of their personal opinion.[16] These approaches can help improve the quality of the discussion.[17]

Apply the solution of a similar problem

You might wonder how to jump-start your idea generation. Well, to begin with, you can learn from others who are in your field or from problem solvers in different areas whose solutions you can transfer to your problem.

Imagine a high-school principal who wants to speed up the cafeteria's lunch line. She can check if some lines move faster than others, check if lines are now moving slower than before, or look at other schools for best practices to transfer. More broadly, she can also look at other organisations that managed checkout processes – convenience stores, airport check-in lines, or public pools. She can also talk to people who manage crowds in general, such as managers of sports stadiums, amusement parks or shopping malls. But why stop there?

Sometimes you can get ideas from seemingly unrelated sources, such as looking at nature to help with engineering design – a practice called *biomimicry*. That's what the engineers of the famous Japanese bullet train Shinkansen did. Their previous design suffered from harsh sound waves whenever a train left a tunnel at high speed. For inspiration, the design team looked for something in nature that could cope with sudden changes in air resistance. They found that the kingfisher's special beak enables it to dive from air, a low resistance medium, into water, a high resistance medium, with minimal energy loss. This insight inspired the development of the Shinkansen distinctive cone-shaped nose, reminiscent of a kingfisher's beak.[18]

Even though most of the problems we face might look unique on the surface, a biomimicry-inspired approach can be helpful because many problems share structural similarities with other problems, sometimes of a completely different nature. One such common problem is the so-called congestion one. 'Congestion' refers to a mismatch between something that we want more of with something we want less of. Our profitability problem is a congestion one (we want more revenues and less costs). The structure of that *how* map may provide a useful blueprint to address problems that look completely different but have a similar structure (so-called *isomorphic* problems), such as fitting cars in our parking lot or helping Louis XIV with his fountains (see Chapter 1).[19]

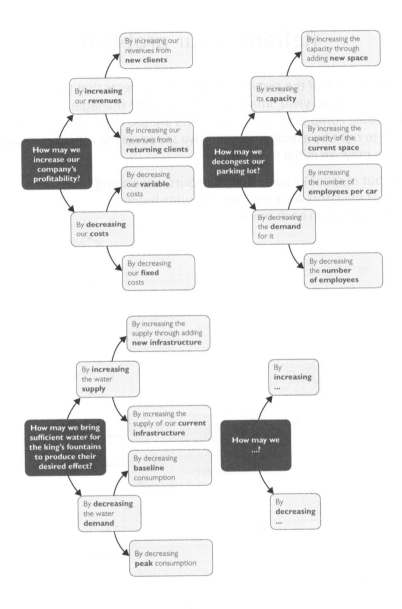

Reframe your problem

To illustrate some of the significant reframing effects that the right-to-left way of ideation can yield, imagine that you're the manager of a building where people complain that the elevators are too slow. Initially, you might start left to right by asking: *'How may we speed up the elevators?'* Take a minute to draw an initial *how* map.

Maybe your map looks something like ours, separating the current elevators from adding new ones before diving into details in each branch.

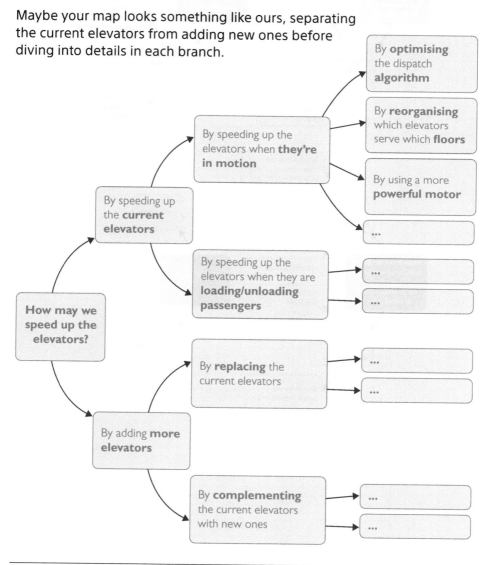

However, with now switching to right-to-left idea generation, you might find your initial framing overly constraining. For instance, it might occur to you to distract elevator users to make them *feel* that the elevators are speedier. How? Well, there are many ways: give them a TV to look at, a mirror in which they can admire themselves, a newspaper they can read, a radio station they can listen to, an internet access on which they can surf the net – you name it.[20] The bottom line is: None of these ideas would fit in your original *how* map.

Now, if you believe that this line of thinking might be worth pursuing, you can go back and broaden the quest so that it accommodates these and other options. For instance, you might reframe your quest to state: *'How can we make our users happy with the speed of our elevators?'* This new line of thinking opens fantastic avenues; after all, installing a few mirrors would cost a lot less than swapping the elevators' motors or installing new elevators!

The key point is that sometimes, an (in this case) engineering problem isn't best solved with an (in this case) engineering solution. Reframing our problem in a broader or a narrower scope can drastically improve our problem solving. And although this idea might look trivial, make no mistake, seeing that your current frame is overly narrow or broad is usually far from trivial.

A second observation is that problem framing and option generation are closely interlinked. One informs the other and it can therefore pay off to iterate between the two as new evidence helps us gain new insights into our problem.

Relax constraints

We all have mental filters that automatically weed out the 'overly crazy ideas' whenever solving a problem. Although these filters help us be pragmatic, they can also interfere with our creativity, leading us to prematurely weed out options because they seem too far out.

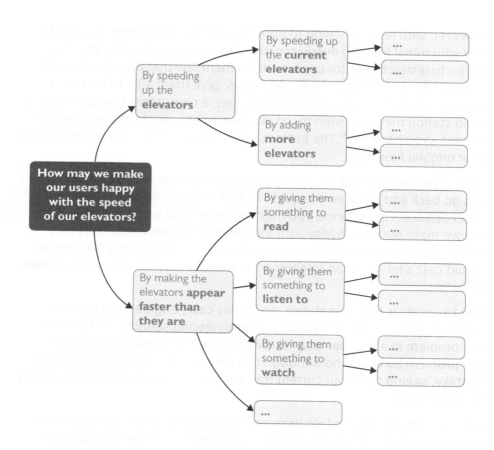

To broaden your option space, think about what holds you back from generating ideas. And then, ask 'what if?' What if we didn't care about cost? What if our key stakeholders were onboard? What if we could partner with our top competitor? Relaxing constraints might take you back to the set-up of your logistics (see Chapter 1). For instance, you might ask: 'What if we had twice or three times the budget?' or 'What if we could work on this problem for six months instead of just four weeks?'

Thinking MECE, we've already exercised our 'what else?' muscle, which helped us identify alternative answers. Asking 'what if?' takes this exercise even further by questioning assumed constraints, the traditional practices that we take for granted because that's how things are done around here. Asking 'what if?' enables you to break free from the straitjackets of convention and habit.

And, to re-emphasise, many of these ideas won't be feasible or desirable. Many will be branded absurd; after all, budgets are limited and getting a project completed on time is important. But, time permitting, there's nothing wrong with having absurd ideas. An absurd idea may be the starting point of a good idea that incorporates the desirability of the absurd idea with the feasibility of something more realistic to implement.

Combine the left-to-right and right-to-left approaches

The left-to-right and the right-to-left approaches to idea generation are not mutually exclusive but, rather, complementary. So it usually pays off to combine them. If you start with a laundry list, at some point structure your ideas to clean up the list by eliminating overlapping or even identical ideas. Similarly, if you start with a structure, you will inevitably wonder at some point how to generate further ideas within a specific category. Then, it is useful to not just rely on logic but to tap into bottom-up tools – such as brainwriting – to develop ideas.

No matter what your preferred approach, you need to manage an important tension: On the one hand, you want to shepherd the process through, building momentum in your problem-solving process. On the other hand, you also want to have the patience necessary to appreciate the value of bad ideas. Why? Because it is often impossible to determine at the outset if an idea is absurd.

Even seemingly absurd ideas might contain the seed for something great, so give your subconscious time to do its job. In fact, research has shown that creative ideas tend to pop up seemingly out of nowhere when you are doing something completely different, such as taking a shower, exercising, meditating or dreaming.[21] For instance, Berkeley neuroscientist Matthew Walker explains that our brains make non-obvious connections during the

REM phases of sleep that lead to unexpected creative insights.[22] Wanna solve that tough problem? Sleep more, take more showers, or do whatever else that relaxes you!

Decide when to quit looking

So, you need to explore different options, which will help you avoid premature closure. But exploring options could go on indefinitely! After all, you can never be sure that your option set is collectively exhaustive. Time is scarce in most problem-solving projects, so when should you stop looking?

Exploration is looking for new options that are unproven but might be potentially rewarding; *exploitation* is sticking with an available good option. There is no known optimal solution for the explore-exploit dilemma, and a general solution might not even exist.[23] However the literature provides some insights.

We often restrict our search to a subset of potential solutions, particularly when our experience is not rich enough to guide our search.[24] So it might be useful to evaluate the diversity of your options: If all of them are of the same kind, or closely related, you may want to continue challenging yourself.

How long to spend searching also depends on the cost of opportunity: What else could you be doing if you were not spending more effort on exploring? If further exploration comes at the expense of thinking through the decision or convincing stakeholders, both of which are critical and time consuming, now might be a good moment to move on. Note, however, that we often see managers close off their search quickly – arguably much too quickly. These observations are in line with research findings on exploration without reward.[25]

Conversely, some teams are reluctant to stop exploring. The hope, whether conscious or not, is that more exploration will lead them to discover a magic bullet that will only have upsides. In our experience, however, magic bullets don't exist – no matter how much exploration is involved. Rather than focusing on finding an alternative that would entail no trade-offs, teams might be better off working through the trade-offs. Realising that the alternatives on the table are the only ones there are can help the team shift from exploration to the next step.

In sum, it might be beneficial to remember that you will probably be better served spreading your limited time to get to a good-enough result for each of the frame, explore, and decide activities than investing it all in one of the three and leaving the other two barely thought through.

USE YOUR OPTIONS TO CREATE ALTERNATIVES

Now that your divergent thinking has fuelled the development of your *how* map, it might contain 20, 30 or even more ideas with varying degrees of detail. Because you've included all ideas independently of their desirability, some of these options are more promising than others. And even though you do not want to make a final call right away on which solution to implement (we'll do so in Chapter 6), it is helpful to converge your thinking onto a manageable set of concrete alternatives that you can evaluate. This is where exploring switches from divergent thinking to convergent thinking.

What constitutes a good set of alternatives is somewhat problem dependent, but a few general rules apply:

- **Each alternative is a logically valid answer to the question.** Each alternative has the potential to answer the full problem without needing the support of another alternative. To take up an already familiar example, re-skim the box on page 64: In Peugeot's case, since the question asks how to fulfil distribution needs, defined as selling and providing maintenance, each alternative must be a complete distribution solution. So 'by selling only' wouldn't be a valid alternative, because it only addresses the selling part of the challenge but gives no direction on how to distribute.

  Note that an alternative may be composed of a collection of fractional solutions, each of which might be small but, as a whole, constitute a group that gets the job done.[26] So it might be that an alternative to increase your profitability will be increasing revenues from return clients in one of your target markets *and* reducing your variable costs for one line of product.

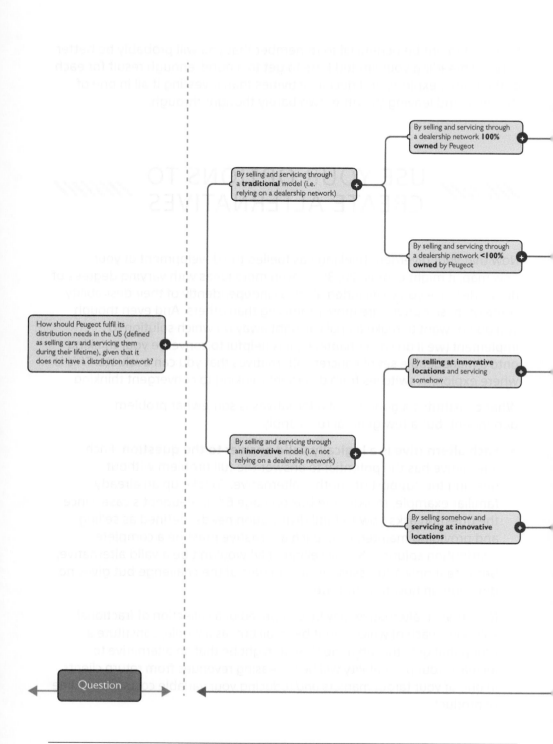

How should Peugeot fulfil its distribution needs in the US (defined as selling cars and servicing them during their lifetime), given that it does not have a distribution network?

By selling and servicing through a **traditional** model (i.e. relying on a dealership network)

By selling and servicing through a dealership network **100% owned** by Peugeot

By selling and servicing through a dealership network **<100% owned** by Peugeot

By selling and servicing through an **innovative** model (i.e. not relying on a dealership network)

By **selling at innovative locations** and servicing somehow

By selling somehow and **servicing at innovative locations**

Question

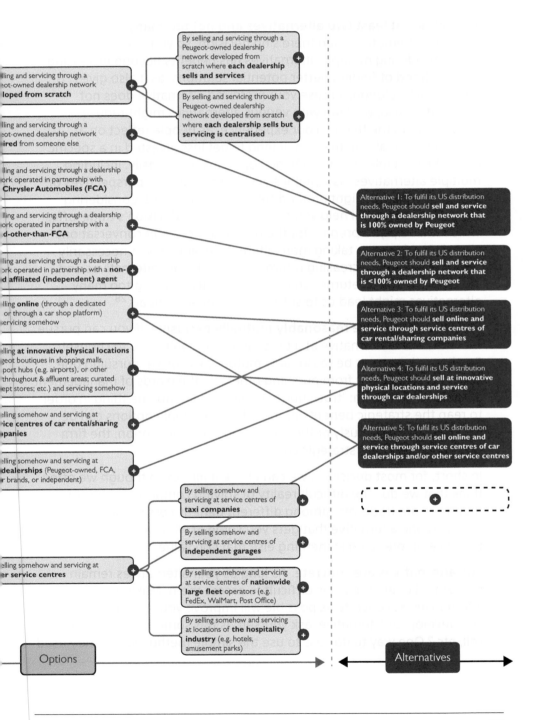

- **The set has at least two alternatives and not too many**. If you only have one alternative, then there's no decision, so you need at least two. Considering multiple alternatives has benefits beyond increasing the likelihood of finding better potential solutions, as it also gives you fallback solutions in case your preferred alternative does not work out.[27] Also, working with various alternatives might reduce politics within the team. In our experience, as people reflect on a wider range of alternatives, they tend to get less invested in a specific one, which enables them to change opinions more easily. Including multiple alternatives also enables you to integrate the perspectives of stakeholders who might prefer different ways forward. Considering their preferences will help you think through the decision's trade-offs, which will help you prepare for the potentially difficult conversations ahead. But, beware: taking more alternatives ahead isn't necessarily better. There are decreasing returns to having more alternatives and, at some point, the returns can become negative: having too many alternatives might lead us to suffer from choice overload.[28]

- **The alternatives are reasonably mutually exclusive**. If you can pursue more than one alternative at a time, then you don't need to choose! So alternatives must be reasonably mutually exclusive: pursuing one should preclude you from pursuing others. In the words of management scholar Roger Martin: 'true choice requires giving up one thing in order to reap the strategic benefits of the other. If multiple options can be pursued simultaneously or there is but one sensible option, the firm does not face a true strategic choice.'[29]

  In short, for most decisions, we can't have it all – even though we often think that we do. The difficult reality of solving complex problems is that there are trade-offs among different benefit-cost constellations: pursuing one alternative that gets you some of what you value comes at the price of foregoing something else that you value.

- **The alternatives are concrete**. As long as your alternatives remain conceptual or abstract, it is difficult to assess them. Making your alternatives as concrete as possible will improve your thinking. When you develop an alternative, ask yourself: Is this something I can do, buy, sell, etc.? One way to do so is to use the simple method we already used in framing our problem: show your prototype alternative to someone unfamiliar with it. Ask them to read it out loud in front of you so you can see where they're struggling, and ask them to explain it back to you after reading it only once so you know if it's concrete enough.

- **The alternatives are promising**. Developing our *how* map, our goal was to create lots of options. Obviously, we won't be able to implement all of them; in fact, we might not even want to. Although our formal evaluation will take place in the next step, we can already start filtering out the solutions that do not look promising now. When converting options into alternatives, throw out those that are obviously either not feasible or desirable. Validate that you have real alternatives (not pseudo alternatives that make the real alternative look better in comparison). Also, throw out those that look overly similar. In our experience, if team members disagree about alternatives, you probably are in good shape.[30] As a rule of thumb, keep looking for alternatives until you or your team members fall in love with at least two.

In practice, alternatives can come from anywhere in your map. To help conceptualise this, consider an analogy: our quest is to prepare a great dish for our dinner guests. In this analogy, the options in the map are the ingredients that we have to prepare the dish. Our map helps us account for each exactly once (we don't forget any, we don't double-list some). And the alternatives are the recipes. So, our decision is to find the recipe that we think will work best. Some recipes (alternatives) might use one single ingredient (option) whereas others use various.

///////// CHAPTER TAKEAWAYS /////////

Don't run off implementing whatever alternative first occurs to you. Instead, as everywhere else in the process, start with divergent thinking. You can do so by developing a *how* map in which you systematically identify and organise the various ways of solving your problem.

Good *how* maps follow the same four rules as good *why* maps:

- Mapping rule 1: They answer a single *how* question.

- Mapping rule 2: They go from the question to potential solutions.

- Mapping rule 3: They use a MECE structure.

- Mapping rule 4: They are insightful.

Don't let thinking MECE and insightful get in your way! If you can't think of a great structure for your map, no problem, start by developing a laundry list of ideas. In the end, your *how* map does indeed need to have a MECE and insightful structure, but that doesn't mean that you need to start with the structure.

Don't develop solutions on your own if you can involve stakeholders; in fact, aim to co-create the solution space!

Don't auto-censure too much: a *how* map is useful to explore the solution space. By definition, it will include lots of dumb ideas, and that's fine. Use the map to ideate, keep the evaluation for later.

///////// CHAPTER 4 NOTES /////////

1 See, for instance, Richards, L. G. (1998). *Stimulating creativity: Teaching engineers to be innovators*. FIE'98. 28th Annual Frontiers in Education Conference. Moving from 'Teacher-Centered' to 'Learner-Centered' Education. Conference Proceedings (Cat. No. 98CH36214), IEEE.

2 See Bouquet, C. and J. Barsoux (2009). 'Denise Donovan (A): Getting Head Office Support for Local Initiatives.' *IMD Case Series IMD-3-2103*, Lausanne, Switzerland.

3 Alternative- vs. value-focused thinking. Although FrED isn't linear, we offer to explore alternatives before exploring criteria (what is called 'value-focused thinking'). Both approaches are valid. For more, see p. 55 of Goodwin, P. and G. Wright (2014). *Decision analysis for management judgment*, John Wiley & Sons; Keeney, R. L. (1992). *Value-focused thinking: A path to creative decision making*. Cambridge, Massachusetts, Harvard University Press; Wright, G. and P. Goodwin (1999). 'Rethinking value elicitation for personal consequential decisions. *Journal of Multi-Criteria Decision Analysis* **8**(1): 3–10.

4 Divergent and convergent thinking occur at all stages of the problem-solving process. See Basadur, M. (1995). 'Optimal ideation-evaluation ratios.' *Creativity Research Journal* **8**(1): 63 –75.

5 See, for instance, Siemon, D., F. Becker and S. Robra-Bissantz (2018). 'How might we? From design challenges to business innovation.' *Innovation* **4**.

6 UN News. (2019). 'Teen activist Greta Thunberg arrives in New York by boat, putting 'climate crisis' in spotlight.' Retrieved April 21, 2021, from https://news.un.org/en/story/2019/08/1045161.

7 See Girotra, K., C. Terwiesch and K. T. Ulrich (2010). 'Idea generation and the quality of the best idea.' *Management Science* **56**(4): 591–605.

8 Let me tell you everything that's wrong with you. One possible explanation as to why dissent helps improve outcomes is that people tend to be more demanding when evaluating arguments than they are when formulating them. Therefore, the more debate and conflict between opinions, the more argument evaluation prevails over production (Mercier, H. (2016). 'The argumentative theory: Predictions and empirical evidence.' *Trends in Cognitive Sciences* **20**(9): 689–700).

9 Hong, L. and S. E. Page (2004). 'Groups of diverse problem solvers can outperform groups of high-ability problem solvers.' *Proceedings of the National Academy of Sciences of the United States of America* **101**(46): 16385–16389.

10 For a brief discussion, see Bang, D. and C. D. Frith (2017). 'Making better decisions in groups.' *Royal Society Open Science* **4**(8): 170–193.

11 Horwitz, S. K. and I. B. Horwitz (2007). 'The effects of team diversity on team outcomes: A meta-analytic review of team demography.' *Journal of Management* **33**(6): 987–1015.

12 See p. 61 of National Research Council (2011). *Intelligence analysis for tomorrow: Advances from the behavioral and social sciences*. Washington, DC, National Academies Press.

13 Bang, D. and C. D. Frith (2017). 'Making better decisions in groups.' *Royal Society Open Science* **4**(8): 170–193. Schulz-Hardt, S., F. C. Brodbeck, A. Mojzisch, R. Kerschreiter and D. Frey (2006). 'Group decision making in hidden profile situations: Dissent as a facilitator for decision quality.' *Journal of Personality and Social Psychology* **91**(6): 1080–1093.

14 See, for instance, pp. 64–66 of National Research Council (2014). *Convergence: Facilitating transdisciplinary integration of life sciences, physical sciences, engineering, and beyond*. Washington, DC, The National Academies Press.

15 Keum, D. D. and K. E. See (2017). 'The influence of hierarchy on idea generation and selection in the innovation process.' *Organization Science* **28**(4): 653–669.

16 See, for instance, Herbert, T. T. and R. W. Estes (1977). 'Improving executive decisions by formalizing dissent: The corporate devil's advocate.' *Academy of Management Review* **2**(4): 662–667.

17 Greitemeyer, T., S. Schulz-Hardt, F. C. Brodbeck and D. Frey (2006). 'Information sampling and group decision making: The effects of an advocacy decision procedure and task experience.' *Journal of Experimental Psychology: Applied* **12**(1): 31.

18 Lim, C., D. Yun, I. Park and B. Yoon (2018). 'A systematic approach for new technology development by using a biomimicry-based TRIZ contradiction matrix.' *Creativity and Innovation Management* **27**(4): 414–430.

19 This is called analogical problem solving; for a primer, see Holyoak, K. J. (2012). Analogy and relational reasoning. *The Oxford handbook of thinking and reasoning.* K. J. Holyoak and R. G. Morrison. New York, Oxford University Press**:** 234–259. Kahneman, D. and D. Lovallo (1993). 'Timid choices and bold forecasts: A cognitive perspective on risk taking.' *Management Science* **39**(1): 17–31. Gick, M. L. and K. J. Holyoak (1980). 'Analogical problem solving.' *Cognitive Psychology* **12**(3): 306–355. See also pp. 99–119 of Epstein, D. (2020). *Range: How generalists triumph in a specialized world*, Pan Books. Lovallo, D., C. Clarke and C. Camerer (2012). 'Robust analogizing and the outside view: Two empirical tests of case-based decision making.' *Strategic Management Journal* **33**(5): 496–512.

20 See p. 25 of Mason, R. O. and I. I. Mitroff (1981). *Challenging strategic planning assumptions: Theory, cases, and techniques*, Wiley New York.

21 For more on creative problem solving techniques, see p. 23 of Reeves, M. and J. Fuller (2021). *Imagination machine: How to spark new ideas and create your company's future*, Harvard Business Review Press.

22 For a summary of the impact of sleep on human functioning (including creativity), see Walker, M (2018). *Why we sleep*, Penguin. For a more detailed study on the role of sleep for ideation, see Gish, J. J., D. T. Wagner, D. A. Grégoire and C. M. Barnes (2019). 'Sleep and entrepreneurs' abilities to imagine and form initial beliefs about new venture ideas.' *Journal of Business Venturing* **34**(6): 105943.

23 Explore/exploit and optimise/satisfice. Nobel Prize laureate Herbert Simon coined the term satisficing by combining satisfying and sufficing. We satisfice when we stop looking for a solution after we've identified one that is good enough. This contrasts with optimising, which consists of always looking for a better solution (Simon, H. A. (1990). 'Invariants of human behavior.' *Annual Review of Psychology* **41**(1): 1–20). Our drive to be collectively exhaustive relates to optimising, but we can never be sure that we are collectively exhaustive (because no matter what we've identified, there might be another possibility out there). Cohen, J. D., S. M. McClure and A. J. Yu (2007). 'Should I stay or should

I go? How the human brain manages the trade-off between exploitation and exploration.' *Philosophical Transactions of the Royal Society B: Biological Sciences* **362**(1481): 933–942. Song, M., Z. Bnaya and W. J. Ma (2019). 'Sources of suboptimality in a minimalistic explore–exploit task.' *Nature Human Behaviour* **3**(4): 361–368.

24 Sanborn, A. N. and N. Chater (2016). 'Bayesian brains without probabilities.' *Trends in Cognitive Sciences* **20**(12): 883–893.

25 Exploration without reward, the secretary problem. An interesting subset of the explore/exploit dilemma is when exploration doesn't provide any reward, a situation known as the secretary problem. Imagine a searcher (employer) interviewing secretarial candidates one at a time. The searcher's goal is to identify the single best candidate. After each interview, the searcher must decide whether to make an offer. If the offer is made, the exploration ceases. If the searcher doesn't make an offer, there won't be a chance to make that offer again to the candidate later. How many candidates should the searcher interview before making an offer? An optimal solution exists: 37%. The searcher should *not* make an offer to the first candidates but, instead, use them to calibrate expectations. Then, after interviewing the first 37% candidates, the searcher should make an offer to the first candidate who is better than any the previous ones. In one study, participants at first failed to search long enough but learned to extend their search in subsequent trials. See Sang, K., P. M. Todd, R. L. Goldstone and T. T. Hills (2020). 'Simple threshold rules solve explore/exploit trade-offs in a resource accumulation search task.' *Cognitive Science* **44**(2): e12817; Seale, D. A. and A. Rapoport (1997). 'Sequential decision making with relative ranks: An experimental investigation of the "secretary problem".' *Organizational Behavior and Human Decision Processes* **69**(3): 221–236.

26 A collection of piecemeal solutions also works. Talking at a recent event at IMD, Swiss explorer Bertrand Piccard called these piranha solutions because each, on its own, would take a long time to get the job done but, as a group, they are extremely effective.

27 Alternatives come in all numbers. For some problems – so-called choice problems – the set of alternatives is naturally small and finite; for others, it might be large or perhaps infinite, as is the case in design or optimisation problems (Wallenius, J., J. S. Dyer, P. C. Fishburn, R. E. Steuer, S. Zionts and K. Deb (2008). 'Multiple criteria decision making, multiattribute utility theory: Recent accomplishments and what lies ahead.' *Management Science* **54**(7): 1336–1349).

28 More choice is not necessarily better: no matter whether it's salad dressings in the supermarket, stereo systems at the consumer electronics store, or colleges to go to, too many alternatives can lead to detrimental outcomes as our mental decision system gets overloaded. For an excellent overview of negative implications of having too much choice, see Schwartz, B. (2005). *The paradox of choice*, Harper Perennial. Schwartz, B. (2004). *The paradox of choice: Why more is less*, New York, Ecco New York.

29 Martin, R. (1997). Strategic choice structuring: A set of good choices positions a firm for competitive advantage.

30 Can we disagree, please? During a meeting where the top management of General Motors was considering a difficult decision, chairman Alfred P. Sloan made a final comment, 'Gentlemen, I take it we are all in complete agreement on the decision here?' He waited for each person to confirm. 'Then, I propose we postpone further discussion of this matter until our next meeting to give ourselves time to develop disagreement and perhaps gain some understanding of what this decision is about.' (Burkus, D. (2013). 'How criticism creates innovative teams.' *Harvard Business Review Blog.*)

Chapter Five
—

Clarify what matters – Explore criteria

So far, in Part 2 you have explored alternatives. This chapter shows you how to explore criteria that you can use to evaluate these alternatives. You will learn to identify what matters to you and to your stakeholders so that you can deliberately weigh off an alternative's benefits and drawbacks. You'll also learn how to prioritise criteria so that they best represent the group's viewpoint.

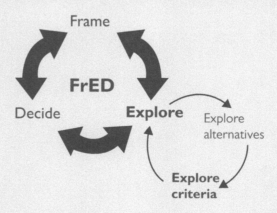

Picture this: You face a difficult decision that requires agreeing with one of your colleagues, and it looks like you won't agree. You have scheduled a meeting where you hope to reach common ground. Before the meeting, you remind yourself to be open minded and you commit to seeing the situation from her viewpoint. But once the meeting starts, your colleague states right away what he wants to do and why. You counter with your preferred alternative, revealing an unbridgeable gap. Both of you dig in your heels, emotions dial up to 11, and you get nowhere. It's a stalemate.

All too often we quickly jump into defending the alternative we prefer. This is what Center for Applied Rationality's Julia Galef calls a *soldier* mindset.[1] But our intuitive judgment improves much if we delay choosing until the end of a structured process.[2] Therefore, it is advisable to start with an open mind or, as Galef calls it, a *scout* mindset. Part of this open-mindedness is developing various alternatives, which we did in the previous chapter. Another part entails expressing what matters to us as we get our treasure – our decision criteria.

Making strategic decisions requires pursuing competing objectives and, thus, inevitably involves making trade-offs.[3] For instance, you might be developing a go-to-market strategy for a new product that must be effective *and* low-cost *and* aligned with your organisational values. As a result, you will need to give away something that you value for something that you value more. In other words, whichever alternative you select will have a cost. Realising that there is no free lunch is a good reminder that if something seems too easy in the decision process, you're probably missing something.

If an alternative seems too good to be true, it probably is

We worked with the 20 most senior executives of an organisation from the travel industry on an innovation exercise. It was an intensive multi-day programme during which the teams were furiously developing new offerings. One morning, after a long night of work, one team showed up, grinning. 'We did it', they boasted, 'we found an offer that looks great on all criteria!' 'That's fantastic', we replied. 'Just one question: if it's so good, why haven't you already done it?' Their reply was immediate, 'Well, our CEO would never go for it'. And then they stopped, processing what they had just said.

It took them a minute to realise what was going on. With further probing, they realised that they had forgotten to consider whether the initiative fitted with the overall strategy and implementation risks that were high on the CEO's agenda. So they went back to the drawing board, refining their recommendation using the newly surfaced criteria.

Like you and us, these were smart, hardworking people who had spent significant time working on their challenge. And yet, they missed something fundamental. We bring up this example to highlight that it isn't entirely obvious to integrate all the relevant criteria, yours and those of your key stakeholders. Rather, it takes a conscious effort.

Just like we have a tendency to settle too early for a limited set of alternatives, we naturally think of only a portion of the evaluation criteria. We *think* we know what we want, but a closer examination often shows us wrong. Now, to be fair to ourselves, criteria don't just pop up in neat lists, and complex decisions often require deep soul searching and iterating between the question, the alternatives, and the criteria. Furthermore, what matters differs from one stakeholder to another, so there is often not one objectively superior alternative. This is worth repeating: Complex problems do not have one right answer, only better (and worse) ones.[4] We are not solving for the right answer, we're solving for an excellent alternative or, at least, an acceptable one.

So, let's look at what makes a good set of criteria and how we can develop it. The good news is that we can leverage some of the tools from previous chapters, as a good set has criteria that are reasonably collectively exhaustive, mutually exclusive, and insightful.[5]

ASSEMBLE A REASONABLY //// COLLECTIVELY EXHAUSTIVE //// SET OF CRITERIA

A good list has criteria that are distinct from one another, so that you don't double count anything. It is also reasonably collectively exhaustive, so that you don't forget anything important.

A basic universal set of criteria might be *feasibility + desirability* – as you will want to choose an alternative that you *can* implement (feasibility) and that you *want* to implement more than the others (desirability). Although this criteria set applies to virtually all decisions, it remains generic – and it is usually worth clarifying what feasibility and desirability mean for your specific decision.

The (not so) quiet Swiss countryside

Making critical decisions without a comprehensive perspective of what matters to you is a critical pitfall. Even after ten years, one of us (Albrecht) remembers the purchase of a house here in Switzerland on Lake Geneva. It was a tight market with few opportunities to buy anything. He had a set of criteria, including purchase price, number of rooms, construction quality, proximity to schools, size of garden, and so on. When an opportunity arose, he jumped in quickly to close the deal, fearing that if he didn't, someone else would snatch it away. He moved into the house and during the first night, with the windows open, the noise from the highway a few kilometres down below kept him up all night! It was a huge shock, since a good night's sleep, preferably with open windows to let in the fresh breeze, was something he valued highly. He just hadn't acknowledged this criterion clearly enough in his decision-making process.

→

It took massive renovations – moving windows to the back of the house, in fact – to fix this problem! Now, he has the quiet nights with open windows he was looking for all along, but he might have had an easier time had he been more deliberate with his criteria specification at the outset. If nothing else, he would have walked into this situation with his eyes (and ears!) open, and the first night surprise would not have been as unpleasant. Now, you might say that this should have been obvious. Maybe so. What we see over and over again though (with ourselves and others) is that when time pressure and other stressors kick in during critical decision moments, it's challenging to see clearly the things that really matter.

Criteria are not just beneficial to help you choose among alternatives but can also serve as a launchpad for creating new alternatives. Think of the house purchase example: If we had been more explicit about the quietness consideration from the outset, it might have led us to look at other neighbourhoods or even other villages.

Note, however, that you want to keep the size of the set of criteria manageable. It should balance being collectively exhaustive with being parsimonious, which might mean excluding secondary criteria.[6]

SELECT MUTUALLY EXCLUSIVE CRITERIA

Often, criteria overlap. Consider for instance the trip from NYC to London. You might care about leg space, privacy, and comfort. Although all of them are potentially important, you are mixing up conceptual levels. Leg space, for instance, might be a sub-category of comfort. If you consider them as separate criteria on the same conceptual level, you double count some aspects of alternatives, which introduces problems in our weighted sum approach.

Now, in the case of comfort, it is reasonably easy to identify that some criteria overlap. However, with more abstract criteria, such as organisational fit, alignment with cultural values and other similarly intangible notions, it can be more challenging to explore criteria that are conceptually distinct from one another. Nonetheless, it's critical that you create this clarity both for the sake of your problem-solving efforts and for communicating your conclusions later on. If your audience gets confused because you have not been clear in your thinking, they are less likely to trust your judgment and be convinced by your arguments.

How do you go about doing so? By always asking *why* something matters. For instance, you might say, leg space is important to you. *Why*? Because it allows me to stretch out my feet. *Why* does that matter? Because I can avoid cramps. *Why* is that important? Because it helps me be more comfortable during the journey. Here you might stop and say that this is enough specificity and that you don't need to justify why it's important to be comfortable. The act of asking why a few times has helped you move from *instrumental* criteria to *fundamental* criteria. It's those criteria that you ultimately want to use to evaluate your alternatives. As a rule of thumb, if two criteria score similarly across alternatives, you might want to explore if one might be a sub-criterion of the other. If that's the case, clean up the set!

//// SELECT INSIGHTFUL CRITERIA ////

Good criteria shed light on what matters in our solution. Two key characteristics of insightful criteria are that they are unambiguous and measurable. *Unambiguous* means that the criterion is explicitly defined. Consider 'compensation' as a criterion for deciding among job opportunities. Are you just considering base pay, or are you also including annual bonuses, health insurance, retirement benefits, disability insurance, and other ancillary benefits? If you do not explicitly define what comes under 'compensation', various people will have various interpretations, promoting disagreements.

Relatedly, you should also specify how each criterion will be measured. With financial compensation and other readily quantifiable criteria such as price, weight, time, distance and so on, this can be reasonably straightforward.

However, not all criteria lend themselves to this approach. Qualitative criteria, such as cultural fit, happiness, perceived risk and others, require you and your stakeholders to make judgment calls for how to score them.[7] To be clear, there is nothing wrong with making judgment calls, but when presenting your conclusions, you need to be able to explain why alternatives scored high or low in a convincing manner to a potentially critical audience. In these settings, conclusions formed on weaker-quality evidence – say anecdotes, stories, or analogies – will be weaker than those based on 'hard data'.

On a practical note, it is useful to make your criteria all vary in a consistent direction. For instance, where a higher score is consistently better. Such criteria are called *benefit criteria*. Imagine that what matters to us travelling from New York City to London is price, speed, comfort, and greenness (absence of emissions). The latter three – speed, comfort, and greenness – are *benefit criteria*: for each, an alternative with a higher score is more desirable than one with a low score. But price isn't. With price, a higher price creates a *worse* alternative. There's an easy fix, though: all we have to do is replace 'price' by 'affordability'. Although seemingly trivial, making all criteria benefit criteria will save you headaches when calculating overall scores, interpreting results, and discussing viewpoints with stakeholders.

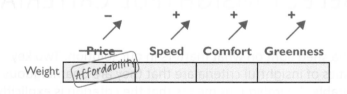

Finally, specify an appropriate range for each criterion. A good way to do this is to develop a 0–100 scale for each criterion. So, if we continue with our NYC-to-London example, an alternative scoring 0 in affordability would be the most expensive one. But don't leave it as such a qualitative description. Instead, define what that means for you. Maybe it's $1000, maybe it's $100k, depending on your viewpoint. What matters is that you be as unambiguous as possible, using quantitative measures in lieu of qualitative ones wherever possible.

	Affordability	Speed	Comfort	Greenness
0	>$20k	>7d	Death possible	>3t CO_2 emissions
25	<$10k	<7d	Significant pain	<3t CO_2 emissions
50	<$7k	<1d	Possible pain	<1t CO_2 emissions
75	<$1k	<8hrs	Some discomfort	<0.5t CO_2 emissions
100	<$.5k	<3hrs	No discomfort	≤0t CO_2 emissions

HOW TO IDENTIFY GOOD CRITERIA

If you're still making fun of Albrecht for omitting to consider quietness when choosing his house, thinking that developing a good list of criteria can't be *that* hard, be careful. In empirical studies, researchers at Duke and Georgia Tech have demonstrated that decision makers can omit nearly half of the criteria they would later consider relevant. Not only that, the participating decision makers perceived the omitted criteria as not only relevant, but almost as important as the criteria they had initially considered![8]

So, identifying criteria might not be as simple as it looks; here are five ideas to help.[9]

- **Take several cracks at it, starting on your own**. Bond and co-authors suggest that you start by yourself, without external help, to get your thinking on paper before it gets influenced by others' opinions. Furthermore, in a series of experiments, they concluded that the best way to improve this general list was to go through the exercise several times (decision makers typically identify only 30% to 50% of their criteria in their first go).[10]

- **Use scenarios**. You may start with listing all relevant and not so relevant concerns that come to mind (you can prune the list later). To make the list more lively, you can turn it into a wish list, a *future perfect* scenario of what would happen if everything went ideally with the problem-solving effort. Why would you be happy with the outcome? Then turn your reasons for happiness into specific criteria. To contrast this positive scenario, also perform a premortem: Assume that your project went wrong and ask yourself why.[11] Maybe your project ended up being too expensive, maybe its outcome was low quality, maybe the implementation was too slow. The goal of these project-yourself-into-the-future techniques is to vividly imagine outcomes prior to the decision to gain further perspective.

- **Leverage frameworks**. Another avenue is to look for frameworks that already provide pre-populated lists of criteria. Take for instance a business-unit manager who is considering where to expand internationally with a new product line. She has identified alternatives: Europe, Latin America or South-East Asia. As she is comparing the three markets, she thinks of their differences and similarities. She considers the levels of competition and how easy or difficult it is to get into the market. As she continues, she remembers that, while in business school, she had learned a framework by Michael Porter, called the five forces framework, that might provide a pre-configured list of criteria she could use.[12] She looks at the list and realises: (1) level of competition, (2) power of buyers, (3) power of suppliers, (4) barriers to entry and (5) threat of substitutes are all relevant criteria that she needs to consider in her market comparison. Digging deeper, she notices that these five criteria cover all of the considerations she had been pondering – in other words, the framework is collectively exhaustive for what she is trying to achieve. Now, could she have developed a similar list by herself? Maybe, but it can be surprisingly difficult to cover all relevant aspects of a challenge just by relying on your own thinking and structuring. So juxtaposing it with other structures, such as those provided by frameworks, can be useful.

- **Contrast alternatives**. Developing criteria in a vacuum might result in a set that misses key trade-offs. In fact, senior executives often confess that even though they go through the effort of developing a matrix, it does not capture the key aspects of their challenges. One main reason seems to be that they often develop their criteria without considering a concrete alternative. As a result, although the criteria look good on paper, they don't connect to what the managers like and dislike. To avoid this trap, start your criteria search by considering two starkly different alternatives. That will help you identify what you value. First, you might just write down what you like and dislike about each alternative. Next, you can articulate more precisely the underlying criteria.

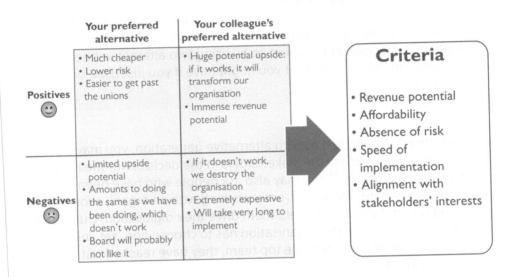

	Your preferred alternative	Your colleague's preferred alternative
Positives 😊	• Much cheaper • Lower risk • Easier to get past the unions	• Huge potential upside: if it works, it will transform our organisation • Immense revenue potential
Negatives ☹	• Limited upside potential • Amounts to doing the same as we have been doing, which doesn't work • Board will probably not like it	• If it doesn't work, we destroy the organisation • Extremely expensive • Will take very long to implement

Criteria

• Revenue potential
• Affordability
• Absence of risk
• Speed of implementation
• Alignment with stakeholders' interests

IMD explores new markets

Consider a discussion we have been having here at IMD, as we think of becoming more active in northern Africa, and more specifically Tunisia. Instead of discussing this idea in the abstract and figuring the criteria to evaluate different market entry approaches, we could also look at two concrete, yet vastly different, alternatives: moving into the Tunisian market as a hub for IMD's activities with our own operations versus moving into the Tunisian market with a local partner who would be running these operations.

Thinking about what we like and dislike about these alternatives helps us quickly surface various issues: going by ourselves has the benefit of control and higher organisational learning but also the downsides of high investments and associated risk, a slow start-up phase, and a lack of market understanding, among others. Partnering would enable us to be fast, limit our investment, and leverage the know-how of our partner. But we would be less in control of the overall initiative, which might put our brand in danger. You get the point.

Looking at concrete alternatives helps envision what we might like and dislike in alternatives. Ultimately, looking at concrete alternatives helps you ask: 'What are the conditions that would have to be true for this solution to be a good one?' Doing so by using two alternatives helps you reduce any blind spots that you might have if you just used one alternative.

- **Enlist others**. Finally, just as with alternative generation, you may want to ask for help. You can ask the stakeholders in the decision for their values, interest, and concerns.[13] You may also ask people who have been in your position elsewhere. We are currently working with an organisation that is looking for an IT provider to help them drive their digitisation. Out of five potential IT providers, the organisation has to choose one. Yet, instead of just setting criteria within the top team, they have reached out to other organisations in Switzerland that are already a step ahead in their digitisation efforts, not to find out which IT provider were chosen, but above all, to understand *how* they made these decisions.

Promote active engagement

Despite your best efforts to engage stakeholders, it might very well be that they don't contribute to their full potential. One key obstacle that can get in the way is Power Distance (PD). The concept of Power Distance captures 'the extent to which the less powerful members of institutions and organisations within a country expect and accept that power is distributed unequally'.[14] Various cultural aspects influence PD, including national cultures. Countries that score high on PD, such as Brazil, France, or Thailand, are more stratified – economically, socially, and politically. This, in turn, means that people accept more readily autocratic leadership styles.[15] Likewise, organisations in these countries tend to have more hierarchical decision-making processes with limited one-way participation and communication.[16]

In an extensive study using data from 421 organisational units of a multinational company in 24 countries, organisational scientists Xu Huang and colleagues found that as Power Distance increased, employees were less likely to speak their mind – a phenomenon known as 'organisational silence'.

The researchers identified two mechanisms that encouraged employees to speak up: First, involving employees in decision-making activities as well as team-building or management-change programmes. Second, and particularly important in cultures with high PD, creating an open and participative climate in which employees perceive that management is supportive of new ideas, suggestions, and even dissenting opinions.[17]

//// PRIORITISE YOUR CRITERIA ////

Finally, not all criteria are equally important, so you need to clarify their relative priority. Say, there is a trade-off to be made between customer satisfaction and cost. How much do you value one over the other? This is a complex enough task, but it gets even more difficult in group decision making, where each stakeholder has an opinion.

Over the past decades, decision analysis has yielded many ways to assign weights to criteria to match the decision makers' preferences. Out of this debate, the community hasn't converged on a single, widely accepted approach.[18] To keep things simple, we propose to follow a simple direct-rating approach where you assign a weight from 1 (weakest) to 5 (strongest) to each criterion.

Weighing is usually an iterative process as your understanding of the problem evolves throughout the process. In particular, you might suffer from equalising bias, the tendency to allocate similar weights to all criteria. To counter this tendency, one debiasing technique consists of ranking the criteria first in numerical order and only then assigning them weights.[19]

//// VALIDATE THAT YOUR CRITERIA //// CAPTURE THE KEY AREAS OF CONCERN

Having come this far, use your list to evaluate alternatives, asking yourself if you would be comfortable living with the resulting decision. If not, you may have overlooked or misstated some criteria: Test whether your criteria would help you explain a prospective decision to someone else. If not, spend more time refining them: What's unclear? What's missing?

///////// CHAPTER TAKEAWAYS /////////

Summarise what matters in a set of criteria that is reasonably MECE and insightful.

For criteria, 'insightful' means that you're balancing being collectively exhaustive and parsimonious; you're giving more weight to the important criteria; you make all your criteria vary in a consistent direction; and you choose an appropriate range of performance for each criterion.

Identifying a good list of criteria can be surprisingly challenging. To help you, consider taking several cracks at it; using scenarios; leveraging frameworks; contrasting alternatives; and enlisting others.

///////// CHAPTER 5 NOTES /////////

1   Galef, J. (2021). *The scout mindset: Why some people see things clearly and others don't*, Penguin.

2   Kahneman, D., D. Lovallo and O. Sibony (2019). 'A structured approach to strategic decisions.' *MIT Sloan Management Review* **Spring 2019**.

3   There are many decision methods out there. There are many decision methods to help people choose when pursuing multiple objectives. Of those, the AHP for analytic hierarchy process (Saaty, T. L. (1990). 'How to make a decision: The analytic hierarchy process.' *European Journal of Operational Research* **48**(1): 9–26) is often cited as one of the most popular. For a review, see Mardani, A., A. Jusoh, K. Nor, Z. Khalifah, N. Zakwan and A. Valipour (2015). 'Multiple criteria decision-making techniques and their applications: A review of the literature from 2000 to 2014.' *Economic Research-Ekonomska Istraživanja* **28**(1): 516–571.

4   Complex problems do not have objectively superior solutions. This is a consequence of their ill-definition. See, for instance, p. 280 of Hayes, J. R. (1989). *The complete problem solver*. New York, Routledge.

5 This aligns reasonably well with others' lists. For instance, 117–118 and p. 121 of Keeney, R. L. (2007). Developing objectives and attributes. *Advances in decision analysis: From foundations to applications.* W. Edwards, R. F. Miles and D. von Winterfeldt, Cambridge University Press: 104–128. For other examples, see p. 50 of; p. 82 of Keeney, R. L. (1992). *Value-focused thinking: A path to creative decision making.* Cambridge, Massachusetts, Harvard University Press.

6 See, for instance, p. 328 of Edwards, W. (1977). 'How to use multiattribute utility measurement for social decision making.' *IEEE Transactions on Systems, Man, and Cybernetics* **7**(5): 326–340.

7 For a more in-depth description of how to do this, see, for instance, pp. 40–42 of Goodwin, P. and G. Wright (2014). *Decision analysis for management judgment,* John Wiley & Sons.

8 Bond, S. D., K. A. Carlson and R. L. Keeney (2008). 'Generating objectives: Can decision makers articulate what they want?' *Management Science* **54**(1): 56–70.

9 For more on this topic, see, for instance, pp. 110–113 of Keeney, R. L. (2007). Developing objectives and attributes. *Advances in decision analysis: From foundations to applications.* W. Edwards, R. F. Miles and D. von Winterfeldt, Cambridge University Press: 104–128.

10 Bond, S. D., K. A. Carlson and R. L. Keeney (2010). 'Improving the generation of decision objectives.' *Decision Analysis* **7**(3): 238–255.

11 Klein, G. (2007). 'Performing a project premortem.' *Harvard Business Review* **85**(9): 18–19. Soll, J. B., K. L. Milkman and J. W. Payne (2015). 'Outsmart your own biases.' Ibid. **93**(5): 64–71.

12 Porter, M. E. (1979). 'How competitive forces shape strategy.' *Harvard Business Review.*

13 See p. 106 of Keeney, R. L. (2007). Developing objectives and attributes. *Advances in decision analysis: From foundations to applications.* W. Edwards, R. F. Miles and D. von Winterfeldt, Cambridge University Press: 104–128.

14 See p. 98 of Hofstede, G. (2001). *Culture's consequences: Comparing values, behaviors, institutions, and organizations across nations*, Sage Publications.

15 Helmreich, R. L., J. A. Wilhelm, J. R. Klinect and A. C. Merritt (2001). 'Culture, error, and crew resource management.', ibid.

16 See p. 16 of House, R. J., P. W. Dorfman, M. Javidan, P. J. Hanges and M. F. S. de Luque (2013). *Strategic leadership across cultures: GLOBE study of CEO leadership behavior and effectiveness in 24 countries,* Sage Publications.

17 Huang, X., E. Van De Vliert and G. Van der Vegt (2005). Breaking the silence culture: Stimulation of participation and employee opinion withholding cross-nationally.' *Management and Organization Review* **1**(3): 459–482.

18 For a review, see Riabacke, M., M. Danielson and L. Ekenberg (2012). 'State-of-the-art prescriptive criteria weight elicitation.' *Advances in Decision Sciences* **2012**. For a good primer on weight assignation, see pp. 44–47 of Goodwin, P. and G. Wright (2014). *Decision analysis for management judgment,* John Wiley & Sons, ibid.

19 Montibeller, G. and D. Von Winterfeldt (2015). 'Cognitive and motivational biases in decision and risk analysis.' *Risk Analysis* **35**(7): 1230–1251.

Part III

—

DECIDE – Select the best on-balance solution

In Part I, we answered 'What's my problem?' Having just answered 'How may I solve my problem?' we're now ready to answer 'How should I solve my problem?' Welcome to Part 3!

Chapter 6 shows how to evaluate alternatives and weigh their trade-offs to identify the best solution. Chapter 7 helps take a step back and, if needed, align additional decisions. Chapter 8 gives ideas on how to summarise your analysis in a compelling message. Finally, Chapter 9 bridges the gap from strategising, which has been the primary focus of this book, to implementing.

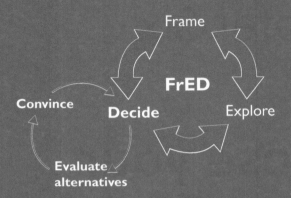

Chapter Six

—

Choose your route – Evaluate your alternatives

It's usually not possible to pursue all alternatives; at least not simultaneously. Many of the important decisions we face are forks in the road, where choosing one path precludes us from pursuing others that might also be attractive. So, after having thought divergently to create potential alternatives, let's think convergently to identify the alternative that would best help us achieve our goals, given limited resources.

Chapter 5 helped us prepare that decision by clarifying what matters to us in an alternative. Because we typically want more than one thing – say, a solution that is fast *and* cheap *and* high quality – and there is usually no alternative that scores best on all counts, we'll need to trade off something that we value for getting a little more of something that we value even more. To be sure, if you have found an alternative with a great score on all criteria, feel free to skip this chapter!

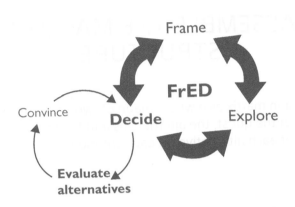

To decide which alternative is best, let's bring the alternatives and criteria together. It's an important step, a bit like at a car factory when the chassis, transmission and engine come together on the production line – a procedure tellingly called 'marriage'. How do we do accomplish a marriage in decision making? Well, a simple decision matrix can be surprisingly helpful, as it incorporates the four components of the decision: the quest that we identified in Chapters 1–3, the alternatives that we obtained in Chapter 4, and the criteria identified in the last chapter. The matrix enables us to systematically evaluate each alternative on each criterion (these evaluations being the fourth component) thereby exposing the alternative's trade-offs and helping us identify which, on balance, works best.

	Criterion 1	Crit 2	Crit 3	Crit 4	Score	Rank
Weight	0.1	0.3	0.5	0.1		
By pursuing (alternative 1)	50	75	100	0	80	1
By pursuing (alternative 2)	25	25	75	25	51	4
...	100	100	25	100	61	3
By pursuing (alternative n)	50	50	75	75	65	2

Quest — How should we do XYZ?
Alternatives
Criteria
Evaluations

ASSEMBLE THE MATRIX'S STRUCTURE

Think of a decision matrix as a whole made of two parts: its *structure* – which consists of the quest, the alternatives and the criteria – and its *inside*, the evaluation of each alternative on each criterion.

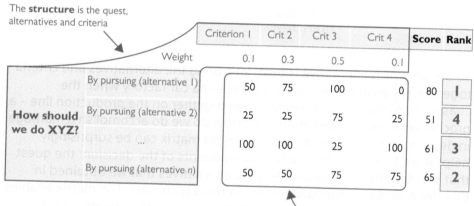

The **structure** is the quest, alternatives and criteria

	Criterion 1	Crit 2	Crit 3	Crit 4	Score	Rank
Weight	0.1	0.3	0.5	0.1		
By pursuing (alternative 1)	50	75	100	0	80	1
By pursuing (alternative 2)	25	25	75	25	51	4
...	100	100	25	100	61	3
By pursuing (alternative n)	50	50	75	75	65	2

How should we do **XYZ?**

The **inside** is the evaluation of each alternative on each criterion

By separating the structure from the evaluations, you delay discussing your preferred alternative. This is valuable because the accuracy of intuitive judgment is improved when people don't make a global evaluation until the end of a structured process.[1]

The preceding chapters helped us assemble the structure; with it in place, let's populate its content.

EVALUATE ALTERNATIVES

Systematically evaluating each alternative is good for two reasons: using one yardstick for all alternatives enables you to be more fair. Also, you create accountability in your thinking vis-à-vis yourself and others.

Given these high returns and how easy it is to use decision matrices, they should be in wide use. And yet we remain surprised by how rarely we see seasoned executives use a matrix to guide their difficult decisions. Some say that it takes too much time, others that it's useless because they can make any matrix turn out the way they want them to. Let's address these critiques in a next step. But first, let's take a look at what kind of evaluations you can use.

Depending on the complexity of your problem and on how much you can invest in solving it, you may want to rely on evaluations that are either qualitative or quantitative.

Qualitative evaluation: In this simple approach, you rate each alternative using a basic scoring system, say from zero to five stars. The approach is so easy to set up that you might do it on the back of a napkin at your favourite restaurant. Such a qualitative matrix can help you and your team get a quick feel for the benefits and drawbacks of the alternatives, which helps surface the major trade-offs.

Although qualitative matrices are easy to set up, their value is limited, primarily because they can't factor in the differences in importance you attach to each criterion. If, as is often the case, you value criteria differently – say, to you, quality is much more important than Affordability – just tallying the number of stars scored by each alternative won't tell you which is on balance the best. In fact, when alternatives tally lots of stars on low-importance criteria, this qualitative evaluation might even be misleading.

Because of their limitations, qualitative matrices are useful for getting an initial sense of the overall trade-offs, but they don't lend themselves to evidence-based decision-making of complex problems. There a quantitative matrix is usually needed.

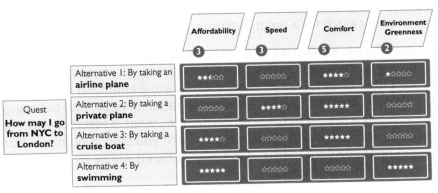

Quantitative evaluation: To gain a better understanding of your alternatives' trade-offs, it is often sensible to evaluate them numerically on each criterion as well as assigning a numerical weight to each criterion, as we discussed in the previous chapter. Doing so enables you to calculate a weighted sum for each alternative.[2] You can do that yourself, or you can use the Dragon Master™ app, which will also colour code the results so that it is easier to see the winning alternative.

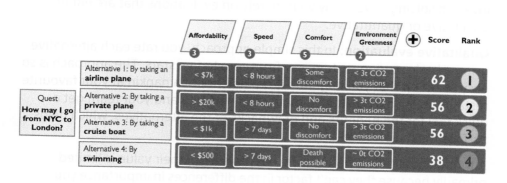

		Affordability (3)	Speed (3)	Comfort (5)	Environment Greenness (2)	⊕	Score	Rank
	Alternative 1: By taking an **airline plane**	< $7k	< 8 hours	Some discomfort	< 3t CO2 emissions		62	1
Quest **How may I go from NYC to London?**	Alternative 2: By taking a **private plane**	> $20k	< 8 hours	No discomfort	> 3t CO2 emissions		56	2
	Alternative 3: By taking a **cruise boat**	< $1k	> 7 days	No discomfort	> 3t CO2 emissions		56	3
	Alternative 4: By **swimming**	< $500	> 7 days	Death possible	~ 0t CO2 emissions		38	4

Note that some managers fall into the trap of focusing on the aggregate score without understanding the sub-scores on each criterion. How you evaluate alternatives on criteria is both a science and an art. It's a science because you use a structured, transparent and verifiable process to break down your problem-solving approach into discrete steps, systematically challenging your thinking at each stage. But setting up a matrix is also an art because there are many choices you make (quite a few implicit ones) on how you gather and evaluate evidence. In the end, your goal is less to find *the objectively right* answer – which most often doesn't exist – as it is to improve the quality of the conversations that you have with yourself and others in your search for a great outcome.

In our experience, executives often make it too much of an art, though, not using an evidence-based analysis for their scoring. As a result, they might not detect their biases. Furthermore, such a casual approach to evaluation means that the support for their recommendation is weak, and believing them becomes a matter of opinion. Remember, what is asserted without evidence can be dismissed without evidence. If you plug in numbers from thin air to populate your matrix, don't expect that it will be as convincing as if you use a verifiable analysis.

Therefore, your challenge is to be as rigorous in your analysis as your limited resources allow you to be. Ask yourself what evidence would be needed to evaluate each alternative on each criterion, be explicit with your assumptions, test your approach with people who disagree with you, and, overall, challenge your assumptions.

In general, you want to argue as solidly as possible for and against each alternative, rather than just look at one perspective.[3] It might be useful to think of yourself as a lawyer preparing to plead a case to a judge – and attempting to make the plea as compelling as possible – but not knowing until the last minute whether you will plead in favour or against the case. It might also be useful to adopt various perspectives, such as organisational, personal, and technical, to gain further insight into your alternatives.[4]

/// MAKE AN ON-BALANCE DECISION ///

Evaluating each alternative on each criterion will help you eliminate those that are clearly inferior across the board. Doing so is straightforward with a quantitative matrix: If alternative A scores below alternative B on all criteria, A is *dominated* by B, and you can safely remove it from further consideration.[5]

Often, though, you will face trade-offs that pose difficult dilemmas. For a recent example, consider how politicians needed to develop a response to Covid that balanced limiting the spread of the virus with limiting the economic damage and psychological distress of locked-down populations. Balancing competing objectives is difficult, but not trying to balance them misses the point. Yes, it is always possible to maximise performance on one criterion but at some point the price paid becomes exorbitant, so decision makers must identify what is reasonable.

The point is that even though you might have diligently followed the FrED process, you are still likely to face difficult dilemmas come decision time. FrED doesn't remove the dilemmas; it merely exposes them.

That seems suboptimal but, still, merely exposing dilemmas is an important contribution, as that makes it easier to seek input from stakeholders to help you refine your question, alternatives, criteria, and evaluations. Also, exposing dilemmas sets the ground to create new alternatives that can help you to bypass the trade-offs (see next section).

Beware of a caveat we raised at the beginning of the section: Numerous executives mention that they can make the matrix produce the outcome that they want simply by adjusting the weights of the criteria and evaluations. 'Sure, you can do this', we reply, 'but committing your thinking to a matrix will enable others to identify your (conscious or unconscious) biases much more easily than if the process took place during a fleeting discussion.' In short, using a matrix makes you more accountable for your thinking.

In our experience, you will often find some discrepancies between your intuitively favoured alternative and the one that scores best in the matrix. If that's the case, investigate these discrepancies. Perhaps some of the criteria aren't sufficiently mutually exclusive? Or maybe an important criterion is missing? For an illustration, go back to the last chapter, where a team thought that they had identified a great alternative, but only because they had missed some key criteria, which they saw through their matrix's results. When they modified their analysis to account for the omission, they reached different conclusions.

Naturally, no amount of analysis can guarantee that your chosen alternative is the best possible one but, as a general rule, it pays off to treat any deviation from your gut feeling as a signal that more analysis is needed. (More on how to manage uncertainty in Chapter 9.)

Generate support by conveying procedural fairness

Not everyone will agree with your decision. Saying yes to one alternative means saying no to many others, which is challenging. As management scholar Richard Rumelt points out: 'There is difficult psychological, political and organisational work involved in saying "no" to whole worlds of hopes, dreams and aspirations.'[6]

Furthermore, given that we don't all value the same things consistently, there will inevitably be important stakeholders who will not agree with your conclusions. We have all experienced disappointing some people in our efforts to achieve the goals we set for our organisation, so we probably all know that just telling people what you have decided can come short.

But, if not that, then, how should you explain your decision? Well, you may want to stress how you've integrated their perspectives in the decision. Research on procedural fairness in courts has shown that defendants are more 'satisfied' with even a relatively severe punishment when they feel that their perspectives were earnestly considered throughout the trial. In other words, people want to know that their side of the story is heard.[7]

What applies to court proceedings may also hold when making complex decisions. To create procedural fairness, integrate others' preferred alternatives and relevant concerns early in the problem-solving process. This will enable you to provide a more balanced account of your final decision, pointing to the strengths of those alternatives that were not chosen.

Beyond demonstrating that you have considered your stakeholders' considerations, also pay attention to how to present your preferred alternative. Research has shown that painting an overly positive picture raises red flags.[8] We agree: We've noticed that painting a balanced picture is particularly important when more junior team members present to senior executives, as it demonstrates that they have grasped the complexity of the issue and understood the underlying trade-offs. Likewise, if you are being presented a recommendation, hearing that the preferred alternative scores best on all criteria should be a signal that something is off. There is no free lunch; if something seems too good to be true, it probably is. So, dig deeper to surface the trade-offs that remains implicit.

Demonstrating your rigour and thoughtfulness doesn't guarantee that everyone will support your solution, of course, but it should improve the odds that even those people who initially opposed your plan support it. That's just one additional reason why investing time upfront is worthwhile, as it can save you time and convincing efforts down the road.

To sum up, your challenge leading the problem-solving effort is to provide direction by deciding what to do while being empathetic, which you can do by conveying procedural fairness. Finding a good balance is delicate: Although you clearly need to invest effort to get your stakeholders on board, you shouldn't over-engage. You face many constraints when solving complex problems – not least limitations on the time that you can invest – and you need to judiciously decide how much engagement serves you best.

TREAT DIFFICULT TRADE-OFFS AS OPPORTUNITIES – INTEGRATIVE THINKING

Max creates his own car to sidestep a difficult trade-off

Max Reisböck was an engineer at BMW in Bavaria in the 1980s.[9] Max and his wife wanted to leave on holidays with the family and their two young children's toys, including bikes and tricycles. As he pondered his alternatives, he faced a difficult trade-off: They could take the family's 3-series sedan, a sportive car that was fun to drive but too small to fit all their stuff. Or they could take their VW estate car wagon, which had lots of boot space but handled a bit like, well, a donkey. In short, they were at a fork in the road. Not a life-or-death situation, yet painful enough for Max to explore whether he could bypass the trade-off altogether.

So, Max became creative. He bought a 3-series sedan, cut off its back, and replaced it with a custom design to create his own estate car. Now called a BMW Touring, Max's car had the best of both worlds: a sportive car that was spacious enough for the family and toys. It was Max's unwillingness to accept the established trade-offs, choosing instead to engage in integrative thinking, that enabled him to create a third way.

Interestingly enough, BMW management had been considering building this type of a car but had held back, thinking that it would not fit BMW's sporty image. When senior managers saw Max's homebuilt model, they were intrigued. In fact, they kept the car at headquarters, and Max had to go on vacation with his VW after all! But they also launched an official project to pursue the Touring, which is now one of the most popular models in BMW's fleet.

Max's insistence to look for a better solution emphasises that as we stand at a fork in the road, it might be worthwhile to explore if the tensions the fork unveils might be a catalyst to develop another alternative. We ought to do this particularly when the trade-offs of the current alternative are too painful to accept.

Management scholar Roger Martin defines integrative thinking as 'the ability to face constructively the tension of opposing ideas and, instead of choosing one at the expense of the other, generate a creative resolution of the tension in the form of a new idea that contains elements of the opposing ideas but is superior to each.'[10]

Each step of FrED promotes integrative thinking: Thinking about your quest, exploring a wide range of alternatives, systematically defining your criteria, and systematically evaluating the alternatives creates a foundation to identify what it would take to resolve trade-offs. In other words, the pain that you feel as you ponder having to choose between one of two imperfect solutions becomes the launch pad for developing a third way. Use the tension to ask: 'How might we create a new alternative using existing building blocks that help us to eliminate the trade-offs?'

Jørgen Vig Knudstorp, former CEO of Lego, stated: 'When you are a CEO, you are sort of forced all the time to have a simple hypothesis. You know there's one answer. But instead of reducing everything to one hypothesis, you may actually get wiser if you can contain multiple hypotheses. You notice trade-offs, you notice opportunities'.[11] By considering multiple alternatives simultaneously, Knudstorp explored opportunities for different solutions. In short, the goal of integrative thinking is to find an answer that takes the best of various alternatives to produce an outcome that is preferable to any of the existing ones.

////// INTERPRET AND CHALLENGE ////// YOUR RESULTS

As you systematically evaluate your alternatives, your matrix highlights the best one. Great! But this isn't the end of the journey just yet. In fact, the output of the evaluation shouldn't be viewed as the solution to your original problem but, rather, as offering a clearer picture of the consequences of choosing one alternative or another.[12] The process so far is a decision aid, but now you need to evaluate how good an aid it is. To help you do so, evaluate the quality of your analysis as a function of the quality of your reasoning and that of your evidence.

You need high-quality reasoning *and* high-quality evidence. In the words of mathematician and physicist Henri Poincaré: 'Science is built up with evidence, as a house is with stones. But a collection of evidence is no more science than a heap of stones is a house.'[13]

So, how do you conduct such a quality check? You have various avenues:

- **Perform a sensitivity analysis.** What happens to the ranking of your alternatives if you modify the weight of your criteria or the evaluations of the alternatives? If small changes result in drastic reordering of the best alternatives, assume that your results are not robust and lower your confidence in them (more about confidence in Chapter 9). If, on the other hand, even sizeable variations in weights and evaluations keep the ranking in order, you might be more confident in your conclusions.[14] Either way, think critically about the 'so what?' of your analysis.

- **Take an external perspective:** It's often easier to give thoughtful advice to others than it is to counsel ourselves. Research on construal-level theory shows that distance can bring clarity.[15] When we are giving advice, we find it easier to focus on the most important factors while our own thinking flits among many variables. In other words, when we think of others we think of the forest, when we think of ourselves, we get stuck in the trees. To attain more distance, ask yourself a few 'what if?' questions. This is exemplified by former Intel CEO Andy Grove who once asked his top team when faced with a difficult decision around terminating an important project: 'What would our successors do?' Doing so helped the team add some distance to the decision.[16]

- **Find a devil's advocate:** Remember Chapter 4 where we highlighted the value of promoting (constructive!) dissent? Now might be another good time for one or two devil's advocates to poke holes into your reasoning. In other words, create a safe environment for the dissenting voices to speak up (see below).

- **Carry out multitrack alternatives if possible:** In our teaching and consulting work, executives often tell us that instead of choosing an alternative they would like to pursue various simultaneously 'to keep their options open'. No doubt, if your setting allows it, this can be an effective approach. By not making a difficult decision that doesn't have to be made, you avoid foregoing other attractive opportunities and you don't face the risk of failing with the alternative you selected. In short, you reduce the risk in your portfolio. As you run test pilots on these multiple alternatives, you can collect additional information and see if your predictions hold. In an increasingly digital world, it is often getting more feasible to run rapid A/B testing that will give you a first understanding of how alternatives perform in real life. Because this can often be done at low marginal costs, multitracking can be one tool to push back the final moment of decision. Beware though that doing so is already a decision in and of itself, so you need to keep the cost of piloting under control. Although the benefit of not committing is that your alternatives are open for longer, you also spread your limited resources across multiple alternatives, which dilutes their effectiveness. You need to assess whether you can afford that dilution.

- **Trust aggregated averages of independent viewpoints over individual estimates:** Consider how many of us book our holiday stays these days. Instead of talking to a single friend who just got back from a wonderful place, we consult travel guides and sites that aggregate user opinions. By consolidating independent viewpoints, these resources give us a more solid base to predict whether that trip to Tuscany will be what we always dreamed of. To be clear, these estimates aren't foolproof – one of us remembers a trip to a restaurant in Rome that had splendid reviews but that turned out to be miserable – but, by and large, aggregating independent data points[17] into large-scale studies can help us form better judgments.[18] Data for your strategic challenge might not always be as easily available as hotel reviews, but if we only have anecdotal evidence of a story someone told us to justify the evaluation of an alternative, we should take it with a grain of salt. Furthermore, note that using various viewpoints to triangulate on what to do is beneficial primarily if the viewpoints are independent.[19] In the end, the quality of our analysis is only going to be as good as the quality of the evidence we can muster up to support evaluation.

Create a safe environment

Psychological safety is the extent to which people on the team feel that they can admit mistakes, voice a dissenting opinion, willingly seek feedback, contribute honest feedback, take risks, or acknowledge confusion without risking being rejected or penalised. Empirical evidence supports that it is a strong predictor of team effectiveness across a variety of organisational context and geographies.[20]

Research also shows that psychological safety is associated with learning, which is particularly relevant in complex and fast-changing environments.[21]

So what? Well, create an environment where dissent is acceptable, in fact, where it's encouraged. In an ideal setting, team members first dissent and then commit to the decision.

/////// CHAPTER TAKEAWAYS ///////

Consistently evaluate each alternative on each criterion. Make these evaluations as rigorous as your limited resources allow you to.

Make your stakeholders feel heard – even if you don't choose their preferred alternative, they should feel that their views were integrated.

Use your decision matrix to improve your sensemaking: identify the 'so what?' of your analysis.

Surface trade-offs. Cases where an alternative scores highest on all criteria are extremely rare, so if that's the case with yours, assume something is off. Likewise, if you are recommended an alternative that only has upsides, treat this as a red flag.

///////// CHAPTER 6 NOTES /////////

1 Kahneman, D., D. Lovallo and O. Sibony (2019). 'A structured approach to strategic decisions.' *MIT Sloan Management Review* **Spring 2019**.

2 Although this simple additive model is very popular, it faces limitations when the criteria aren't fully mutually exclusive. For more on the topic, see, for instance, p. 48, pp. 54–55 of Goodwin, P. and G. Wright (2014). *Decision analysis for management judgment*, John Wiley & Sons. For a review of multi-criteria decision analysis, see Marttunen, M., J. Lienert and V. Belton (2017). 'Structuring problems for multi-criteria decision analysis in Practice: A literature review of method combinations.' *European Journal of Operational Research* **263**(1): 1–17.

3 For discussions, see Lovallo, D. and O. Sibony (2010). 'The case for behavioral strategy.' *McKinsey Quarterly*. See also, pp. 103–104 of Chevallier, A. (2016). *Strategic thinking in complex problem solving.* Oxford, UK, Oxford University Press.

4 Nutt, P. C. (2004). 'Expanding the search for alternatives during strategic decision-making.' *Academy of Management Perspectives* **18**(4): 13–28.

5 See p. 49 of Goodwin, P. and G. Wright (2014). *Decision analysis for management judgment*, John Wiley & Sons.

6 See p. 62 of Rumelt, R. P. (2011). *Good strategy/bad strategy: The difference and why it matters.*

7 See, for instance, Lind, E. A., C. T. Kulik, M. Ambrose and M. V. de Vera Park (1993). 'Individual and corporate dispute resolution: Using procedural fairness as a decision heuristic.' *Administrative Science Quarterly*: 224–251.

8 Friestad, M. and P. Wright (1994). 'The persuasion knowledge model: How people cope with persuasion attempts.' *Journal of Consumer Research* **21**(1): 1–31.

9 For a short description of Max Reisböck's story, see BMW. (2020). 'The seven generations of the BMW 3 series.' Retrieved 29 July, 2021, from https://www.bmw.com/en/automotive-life/bmw-3-series-generations.html.

10 See p. 15 of Martin, R. L. (2009). *The opposable mind: How successful leaders win through integrative thinking*, Harvard Business Press.

11 See p. 8 of Riel, J. and R. L. Martin (2017). *Creating great choices: A leader's guide to integrative thinking*, Harvard Business Press.

12 Riabacke, M., M. Danielson and L. Ekenberg (2012). 'State-of-the-art prescriptive criteria weight elicitation.' *Advances in Decision Sciences* **2012**.

13 See p. 156 of Poincaré, H. (1905). *Science and hypothesis*. New York, The Walter Scott Publishing Co., Ltd. See also pp. 124–131, p. 269 of Gauch, H. G. (2003). *Scientific method in practice*, Cambridge University Press.

14 This is called a 'flat maximum'; see p. 51 of Goodwin, P. and G. Wright (2014). *Decision analysis for management judgment*, John Wiley & Sons.

15 Trope, Y. and N. Liberman (2010). 'Construal-level theory of psychological distance.' *Psychological Review* **117**(2): 440.

16 For the value of an outside-in perspective, see also Kahneman, D. and D. Lovallo (1993). 'Timid choices and bold forecasts: A cognitive perspective on risk taking.' *Management Science* **39**(1): 17–31.

17 The dangers of aggregating viewpoints that aren't independent. Imagine a turkey in a US farm before Thanksgiving (for those of you, dear readers, who are not from the US, the Americans eat a *lot* of turkeys for Thanksgiving). Observing that the farmer feeds it every day, this American turkey might conclude that the farmer is its friend and come to expect that he will continue to feed it ad infinitum. It might also ask the opinion of its fellow turkeys in the farm who, based on the same evidence, might get to the same conclusion: 'yep, the farmer feeds us every day, therefore the farmer is our friend. Expect more food tomorrow.' Unfortunately, for this turkey, reality catches up on Thanksgiving morning. Our turkey might have been better served from forming its opinion by triangulating evidence from independent sources, for instance looking for old turkeys on the farm, to see if there were such a thing as an old turkey, or asking the dog about what happens to turkeys on the farm. For more on Turkey, see pp. 40–42 of Taleb (2007) or refer back to the original, Bertrand Russell's chicken— either way, it unfortunately doesn't end well for the feathered fellows. If the turkey example above illustrates the dangers of pooling biased estimates, Galton's ox helps demonstrate how pooling independent estimates reduces noise. At a village fair, Sir Francis Galton asked 787 villagers to estimate the weight of an ox. Although none guessed the right answer, the average was near perfect (1207 lb estimate for a true weight of 1198 lb). Galton, F. (1907). 'Vox populi.' *Nature* **75**: 450–451. Additional empirical results suggest that combining the opinions of independent agents outperforms the opinion of the best independent agent only when the accuracy of the agents is relatively similar. Kurvers, R. H., S. M. Herzog, R. Hertwig, J. Krause, P. A. Carney, A. Bogart, G. Argenziano, I. Zalaudek and M. Wolf (2016). 'Boosting medical diagnostics by pooling independent judgments.' *Proceedings of the National Academy of Sciences* **113**(31): 8777–8782.

18 This is the principle behind meta-analyses that, although imperfect, provide an excellent standard of evidential quality. See, for instance, Stegenga, J. (2011). 'Is meta-analysis the platinum standard of evidence?' *Studies in history and philosophy of science part C: Studies in History and Philosophy of Biological and Biomedical Sciences* **42**(4): 497–507. Greco, T., A. Zangrillo, G. Biondi-Zoccai and G. Landoni (2013). 'Meta-analysis: Pitfalls and hints.' *Heart, Lung and Vessels* **5**(4): 219.

19 Wallsten, T. S. and A. Diederich (2001). 'Understanding pooled subjective probability estimates.' *Mathematical Social Sciences* **41**(1): 1–18. Johnson, T. R., D. V. Budescu and T. S. Wallsten (2001). 'Averaging probability judgments: Monte Carlo analyses of asymptotic diagnostic value.' *Journal of Behavioral Decision Making* **14**(2): 123–140.

20 See Tannenbaum, S. I., A. M. Traylor, E. J. Thomas and E. Salas (2021). 'Managing teamwork in the face of pandemic: Evidence-based tips.' *BMJ Quality & Safety* **30**(1): 59–63. Frazier, M. L., S. Fainshmidt, R. L. Klinger, A. Pezeshkan and V. Vracheva (2017). 'Psychological safety: A meta-analytic review and extension.' *Personnel Psychology* **70**(1): 113–165.

21 Edmondson, A. C. and Z. Lei (2014). 'Psychological safety: The history, renaissance, and future of an interpersonal construct.' *Annual Review of Organizational Psychology and Organizational Behavior* **1**(1): 23–43.

Chapter Seven

Align interdependent decisions

Aligning decisions at BoKlok

The Swedish prefabricated house manufacturer BoKlok is a joint venture between furniture retailer IKEA and global construction company Skanska. When BoKlok launched operations, central to the business model were decisions the management team to make various interrelated choices, decisions: what types of houses to offer, at what cost point, where to produce them, and how to get to market, to name but a few.

Despite the team's efforts, the initiative failed to take off as expected. As it turned out, the team had failed to determine an appropriate organizational setup between IKEA and Skanska to ensure that the housing units could be produced and delivered in a cost-effective and timely manner. Upon inspection the success of the joint initiative in later years, in short, even the BoKlok management team had co-created many mistakes whose choices had to be made. After missing a single one had dramatic consequences that almost put the entire effort in jeopardy.

Chapter Seven

—

Align interdependent decisions

Aligning decisions at Boklok[1]

The Swedish prefabricated house manufacturer Boklok is a joint venture between furniture retailer IKEA and global construction company Skanska. When Boklok launched operations, making the business model work required the management team to make various integrated choices, deciding what type of houses to offer, at what cost point, where to produce them, and how to go to market, to name but a few.

Despite the team's efforts, the initiative failed to take off as expected. As it turned out, the team had failed to determine an appropriate organisational set-up between IKEA and Skanska to ensure that the housing units would be produced and delivered in a cost-effective and timely manner, which hampered the success of the joint initiative for years. In short, even though Boklok's management team had considered many domains where choices had to be made, their missing a single one had dramatic consequences that almost put the entire effort in jeopardy.

The launch of the IKEA-Skanska Boklok project highlights that decision makers must often integrate decisions in multiple domains of choice when solving complex problems. As strategy scholar Michael Porter pointed out, 'a firm's strategy defines its configuration of activities and how they interrelate'.[2] Part of the challenge is to define upfront the domains where decisions are needed. Often in strategy-setting exercises, top decision makers only focus on one or few domains of choice – say, identifying target markets and product features – leaving the rest to lower levels of the organisation who are meant to execute these high-level decisions. However, if the exercise leaves out critical domains that need to be closely aligned with other decisions – say, setting the speed of implementation, sequencing the strategy roll-out, figuring out partnering approaches – the overall strategy is put at risk because the decisions will eventually be made by lower-rung managers who don't have the big picture perspective required for creating alignment across decisions.

This chapter gives you guidance on how to align interdependent decisions. It also introduces frameworks that may be useful, depending on the nature of your challenge.

IDENTIFY WHERE OTHER DECISIONS ARE NEEDED – LINE UP YOUR BABY DRAGONS

FrED addresses your dragon, but what kind is it? Recall from Chapter 1 that dragons come in two types: big dragons and baby dragons. If FrED is your big dragon, by finding a way to deal with it, you have defined your strategy. But if FrED was just one of the various baby dragons that need to be addressed, you must now address the other baby dragons in the family; that is, you need to make decisions on the other domains of choice that, as a whole, amount to forming a strategy.

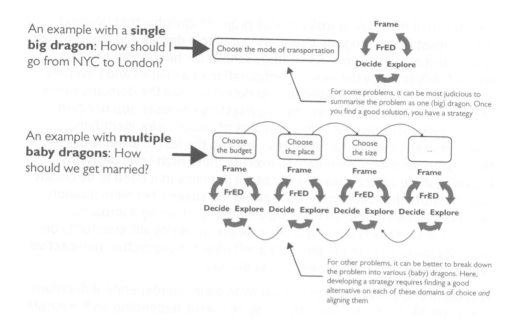

An example with a **single big dragon**: How should I go from NYC to London?

Choose the mode of transportation

Frame
FrED
Decide Explore

For some problems, it can be most judicious to summarise the problem as one (big) dragon. Once you find a good solution, you have a strategy

An example with **multiple baby dragons**: How should we get married?

Choose the budget | Choose the place | Choose the size | ...

Frame | Frame | Frame | Frame
FrED | FrED | FrED | FrED
Decide Explore | Decide Explore | Decide Explore | Decide Explore

For other problems, it can be better to break down the problem into various (baby) dragons. Here, developing a strategy requires finding a good alternative on each of these domains of choice *and* aligning them

Formulate your problem as one big dragon or as a family of baby dragons

Complex problems in general, and setting strategic directions in particular, usually have many moving parts. Effective strategies harmonise these various decisions to transform efforts into outsized results, enabling an organisation to overcome obstacles or making it difficult for others to replicate its success. Consider the case of IKEA: A competitor might be able to copy one part of its value proposition – say, relying on self-assembly of furniture. But emulating IKEA's whole model – using the innovative store layout, providing childcare and restauration, placing stores in optimal locations, employing in-house designers focused on production costs, providing catalogues and so on – is a lot more challenging.[3] Yet it is unclear whether an organisation that didn't provide the fully integrated offer would be competitive. So complex problems are, well, complex and there's only so much complexity that you can remove through clarifications. Then, you have to deal with whatever intricacies are left, however convoluted they remain.

That leaves you with taking one of two routes. Formulating your problem as dealing with a single big dragon is attractive because by going through a single FrED process, you develop your strategy. However, in some settings, this approach can be prohibitively taxing. Imagine creating a *how* map that integrates all the decisions you must make when planning a wedding: how much to invest, where to do it, whom to invite, what food to serve, whether to have live music, what seating arrangements to have for the dinner, and so on.

That *how* map would be massive! It also wouldn't be particularly helpful as you'd struggle to compare alternatives with numerous parts. For instance, how would you compare (a) a wedding set at a remote countryside location with live country music and a BBQ where all of your friends and extended family are invited to (b) a downtown wedding at an intimate luxury hotel with a five-star dinner, inviting only your closest family and friends? Here, it might make more sense to decouple these decisions into baby dragons, first deciding the overall size of the wedding (one baby dragon), and only then moving into other decisions, periodically checking that they support one another or, at least, that they remain compatible.

So, if one approach is to treat your problem as dealing with a single big dragon, at the other end of the spectrum, you can treat it as dealing with a family of baby dragons. Each baby dragon will have its separate FrED, each with its own quest, alternatives, criteria, and evaluations. This approach, no doubt, reduces the complexity of the decision for each individual FrED. But it doesn't address the need for aligning choices across different domains. So, should you treat your problem as one big dragon or a bunch of baby dragons?

Beyond your personal preferences, let the problem guide your approach

In our experience, there is no one-size-fits all. We have thought long and hard about this issue and had many heated debates – this is one of our instances of dissent-and-commit that we're the most proud of! – but the fundamental dilemma of balancing complexity and alignment remains.

So our short answer is 'don't let your personal preference dictate your approach'.

A great golf player doesn't just use the club she prefers but, rather, the one that makes most sense for each shot. Similarly, treating your problem as dealing with one big dragon or with a set of baby dragons shouldn't just be a matter of personal preference.

Although there are no hard and fast rules, answering a few questions might help you choose your approach:

- **Are the decisions you face fairly independent?** If they are, consider treating them as a set of baby dragons. If, on the other hand, they are strongly interdependent, go the big-dragon way as the interdependencies will create incompatibilities that might be hard to manage in a decoupled process (e.g. decisions about products and markets are usually tightly connected.).

- **Is one decision significantly more contested than the others?** If so, it might deserve being a priority baby dragon that you address by itself first. For instance, we just completed a workshop for a large med-tech company where the senior team wanted to chart out a five-year strategy for their business unit. This included decisions about R&D, production, quality, and marketing and sales. Since R&D was a hotly debated domain of choice where the members of the team disagreed, they prioritised this domain, discussing it at length before moving on to the other choices.

- **Is one decision significantly more important than others?** Sometimes there are various decisions required, but settling one brings lots of clarity. To illustrate, management scholar Richard Rumelt offers an example: Imagine that you are running a small grocery shop in the suburbs of LA. Facing increased competition, you must find more customers. You list the actions that can help you: extending opening hours, adding more speciality food for target segments, adding parking and other conveniences, and so on. Considering these choices simultaneously can be overwhelming, as the number of permutations is immense. Instead, it might be more sensible to first make one key decision that would help you in your other choices. For instance, you might decide to first identify the primary market segment you want to serve, say, choosing between (more price-sensitive) students or (more convenience-sensitive) professionals.[4]

Each entails distinct trade-offs and requires different choices. Once you make this high-level decision, you dramatically reduce the complexity of the other decisions. For instance, if you target professionals, it's much easier to decide whether to open more cash registers after 5 pm, whether to add parking spots, whether to modify your product offerings (e.g. substituting munchies with higher-quality food), or whether to limit opening hours.

- **Would full integration result in an overly complex big dragon?** If folding all decisions into one – like in the wedding example above – gives you an intractable problem, you might be better off disaggregating them.

- **Do you need to involve different people in the different decisions?** If so, treating them as baby dragons might make more sense as it will enable you to have all and only relevant people for each decision.

CONSIDER USING EXISTING FRAMEWORKS

Many problems you face are highly specific. For these, you have to define a custom-made strategy that you develop from scratch. Every now and then, however, you might face a more common challenge; here it might be useful to leverage an existing framework from a closely related problem or, leveraging analogical thinking, from a more distance source.

Imagine, for instance, that you are developing a strategy for your organisation. Instead of figuring out from scratch all the baby dragons that you need to address to generate a strategy, you might use Hambrick and Fredrickson's Strategy Diamond model.[5] The model proposes that developing a strategy requires you to make decisions in five key domains: arenas, differentiators, vehicles, staging and economic logic.

If you find that the Diamond model is insightful for the challenge that you're facing, you might use these five domains of choice as a checklist of decisions that you will need to make.

Similarly, imagine that you want to (re-)define the business model for your organisation. Here, Osterwalder and Pigneur's Business Model Canvas (BMC)

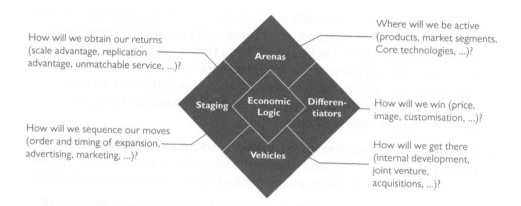

How will we obtain our returns (scale advantage, replication advantage, unmatchable service, ...)? — **Arenas**

Where will we be active (products, market segments, Core technologies, ...)?

Staging — **Economic Logic** — **Differen-tiators**

How will we sequence our moves (order and timing of expansion, advertising, marketing, ...)? — **Vehicles**

How will we win (price, image, customisation, ...)?

How will we get there (internal development, joint venture, acquisitions, ...)?

can be useful.[6] The BMC provides nine domains of choice – partners, activities, resources, cost structure, value proposition, customer relationships, channels, customer segments, and revenue streams – that you can use as a list of the baby dragons that you need to address. Other frameworks that might be useful include Galbraith's Star, Porter's Five Forces, Ansoff's Growth Matrix, SWOT, PESTLE, and others.[7]

Using an existing framework can be immensely useful. By helping you identify what to consider in a decision, it enables you to outsource some of the hard thinking required to a management scholar. However, using frameworks can also be dangerous. A structural weakness of existing frameworks is their lack of insightfulness for the specific problem that you are facing. Since they have not been designed to address your specific challenge, they might include points that are not particularly relevant to you, or they might break down the problem in a way that doesn't add much value. Some widely used frameworks also suffer from a lack of MECEness.[8]

This point is particularly salient, as strategy is often taught in business schools as applying pre-made strategy frameworks. During their MBA, students see two or three dozens of those. Fast forward a couple of years, and they might remember a handful. Give them another couple of years still, and all they remember is two or three – and they will force-fit these frameworks to whichever challenge they face. In the words of psychologist Maslow, 'I suppose it is tempting, if the only tool you have is a hammer, to treat everything as if it were a nail'. Well, we've seen these strategists with their, say, PESTLE hammer trying to use that framework to analyse whatever problem comes their way. Sometimes it works, but in general the result isn't particularly glorious. And because using a framework gives them the illusion that they've done a quality analysis when they haven't, it can be a dangerous practice.

So, should you use an existing framework for your problem? Well, look at it this way: An existing framework is a great servant but a terrible master. If your problem happens to closely resemble one for which a framework has been developed, then, by all means, consider using it. Otherwise, no problem: You now know how to make your thinking MECE and insightful; therefore you can develop your own framework, one that is tailor made for the issue you face. And that, dear reader, is miles ahead of many strategists out there!

/////// CHAPTER TAKEAWAYS ///////

Identify other decisions needed so that your strategy is a consistent whole.

Existing strategy frameworks often do not fully cover your individual requirements. But don't be too focused on adapting the framework to your specific needs; if no existing framework applies well, no problem, just develop your own! 'All' you have to do is think MECE and insightful.

If you're dealing with more than one dragon, align the decisions resulting from each of these analyses so that they are self-reinforcing.

Existing frameworks *may* be great servants but are terrible masters. You can leverage one for assistance, but it's unwise to outsource your thinking to someone who knew nothing about the intricacies of your problem when they devised their framework.

/////// CHAPTER 7 NOTES ///////

1 Burgelman, R. A., M. Sutherland and M. H. Fischer (2019). BoKlok's Housing for the Many People: On-the-Money Homes for Pinpointed Buyers. *Stanford Case SM298A*.

2 See p. 102 of Porter, M. E. (1991). 'Towards a dynamic theory of strategy.' *Strategic Management Journal* **12**(S2): 95–117.

3 Porter, M. E. (1996). 'What is strategy?' *Harvard Business Review*.

4 See pp. 86–87 of Rumelt, R. P. (2011). *Good strategy/bad strategy: The difference and why it matters*.

5 Hambrick, D. C. and J. W. Fredrickson (2001). 'Are you sure you have a strategy?' *Academy of Management Executive* **15**(4): 48–59.

6 See pp. 14–44 of Osterwalder, A. and Y. Pigneur (2010). *Business model generation: A handbook for visionaries, game changers, and challengers*, John Wiley & Sons.

7 For more examples of frameworks see, for instance, Planellas, M. and A. Muni (2020). *Strategic decisions*. Cambridge, Cambridge University Press. Also pp. 72–74 of Chevallier, A. (2016). *Strategic thinking in complex problem solving*. Oxford, UK, Oxford University Press. Also, pp. 109–111 of Baaij, M. and P. Reinmoeller (2018). *Mapping a winning strategy: Developing and executing a successful strategy in turbulent markets*, Emerald Group Publishing.

8 See, for instance, Grönroos, C. (1997). 'From marketing mix to relationship marketing-towards a paradigm shift in marketing.' *Management Decision* **35**(4).

Chapter Eight
—

Win 'em over – Convince effectively

To be effective, even the best analysis can't just rely on its own merits. It must also be expressed in a way that will convince key stakeholders. In this chapter, we shift our attention from reaching solid conclusions to exploring how to synthesise these conclusions into a compelling message.

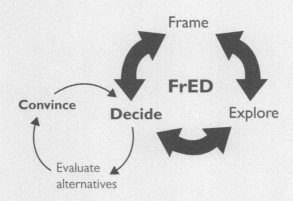

////// DEVELOP A COMPELLING ////// MESSAGE

In an ideal world, we all would be perfectly rational. Then, all it would take would be for you to present your recommendations, explain how you reached them, and to then demonstrate the solidity of your analysis. Your audience would be awed by your professionalism and would support your recommendations.

The reality is that people value different things, so they won't all favour the same solution. In addition, there are hidden agendas behind projects, turf battles, and faulty logic at play. And, as human beings, we are not just guided by our pre-frontal cortex driven rational thinking, but also strongly influenced by our deeply ingrained emotional responses (remember System 1 and System 2 thinking from the Introduction?). All this to say, no matter how brilliant a piece of analysis might be, if all it stands on is its intrinsic validity, it's probably not very compelling. In short, there's often a difference between being right and being effective. And the latter calls for being persuasive.

Persuading others isn't a new sport, and the Classics bring in some resources. Aristotelian persuasion, in particular, relies on three pillars: logos, ethos, and pathos.[1]

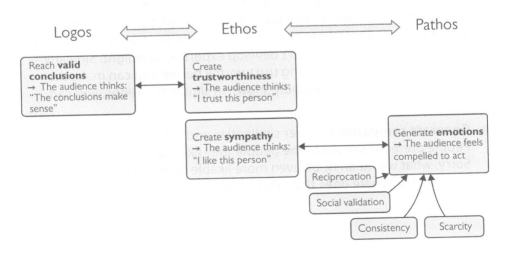

Appeal to logos/logic

Using valid reasoning and high-quality evidence, *logos* – or logic – aims at reaching valid conclusions. The earlier chapters of the book show how you can sharpen your logos using FrED. However, we have not paid much attention yet to the other two pillars, ethos and pathos.

Appeal to ethos/ethics

An appeal to *ethos* consists of creating trustworthiness and sympathy with your audience to increase the likelihood that they accept your arguments.[2]

- **Create trustworthiness.** Beyond using valid reasoning and high-quality evidence, you can demonstrate trustworthiness by skilfully bringing up your expertise. Instead of assuming that your recommendations are self-evident, you might want to explain why you're qualified to make them. You hear such appeals to ethos in statements like 'trust me, I'm a doctor' or 'we, at Harvard, . . . ' You also hear them anytime a speaker is introduced: 'she is a professor at Prestigious University', 'he has been a senior partner for 25 years at Amazing Consultancy', or the ultimate appeal to ethos and display of laziness: 'a man who needs no introduction' (that one only works with people who do not need any introduction indeed). Note that such appeals to trustworthiness require time to build. Just as you can't develop expertise overnight. Similarly, it takes a track record of being trustworthy before you can make the argument: 'as I have repeatedly shown in similar situations, you can trust me.'

- **Generate sympathy.** Uncover similarities and offer genuine praise. People prefer to say yes to the people they like. So, be likable! Sorry, what we mean is, be even more likable than you already are, dear reader. Where does that start? Well, look your best and dress appropriately, for one. As our colleague Phil Rosenzweig exposed, the halo effect is a tendency that we have to allow our overall impression to influence our thinking.[3] Other ways to generate sympathy include making the audience feel that you are concerned about them, that you understand them, and that you have their interests at heart.

Appeal to pathos/emotions

Using *pathos*, you appeal to the emotions.[4] Social psychologist Jonathan Haidt uses the metaphor of an elephant and a rider to highlight the importance of emotions, where the elephant represents our emotional side and the miniscule rider at the top the rational, analytical side.[5] Although the rider can provide direction to the elephant, it is ultimately the elephant that moves and sustains momentum. Similarly, our decisions rely on rational evaluations *and* on our ancient, deeply embedded emotionally driven thinking and feeling mechanisms.[6] This reality isn't necessarily bad, as research shows that feelings and emotions experienced during decision making can have a positive effect on the overall decision performance.[7]

Social scientists have identified various approaches that can help you appeal to the emotions of an audience:

- **Tap into appropriate feelings:** After Apple pushed Nokia out of its leading position in the smartphone market in the late 2000s, former Nokia CEO Stephen Elop had to communicate drastic measures to his organisation. Instead of just showing analytical charts, he used a metaphor to emphasise Nokia's dramatic situation: 'We too, are standing on a "burning platform", and we must decide how we are going to change our behavior. Over the past few months, I've shared with you what I've heard from our shareholders, operators, developers, suppliers and from you. Today, I'm going to share what I've learned and what I have come to believe. I have learned that we are standing on a burning platform. And, we have more than one explosion — we have

multiple points of scorching heat that are fueling a blazing fire. . . '[8]
Now, it is debatable whether Elop's choice of metaphor was appropriate
to produce the change needed to help Nokia build a more successful
future. But the point is that any rational message you convey also
impacts how your audience feels, which, in turn, impacts how they
react, no matter whether you actively address this dimension or not.
Instead of leaving it up to the audience to react however they may,
think of the emotional response you want to create. Is it anger, fear, joy,
excitement, trust, . . . ? And once you have identified what it should be,
craft your message accordingly. Tell a story, use an analogy or work on
your delivery to elicit that emotional response.

- **Generate a need for reciprocation.** Give to receive. As individuals,
  we subscribe to a norm that dictates us to repay in kind what we've
  received, which explains why marketers offer free samples or why
  people make gifts and favours during negotiations. The need for
  reciprocating also gets us to make concessions, so that if we reject a
  large ask, we might accept to make a smaller effort.[9]

- **Use social validation (or peer power).** Although we tend to pride
  ourselves on being independent, in reality what our peers do
  strongly influences us. We've already addressed this behaviour in the
  Introduction, calling it anchoring and labelling it a bug (or bias). But
  that bug can be turned into a feature: If you can get a critical mass of
  people to behave how you'd like, their behaviour will influence others.
  As you get ready to communicate your proposal, identify who you need
  to engage when to create that momentum of support. Peter Block's
  trust-agreement matrix can help you categorise your stakeholders to
  determine how to approach them.[10] In the matrix, trust refers to the
  quality of the relationship you have with each stakeholder, which might
  be the result of previous interactions. Agreement refers to whether
  you and your stakeholders agree on the specific issue at hand. Tailor
  your communication to your stakeholders' positions in the matrix. For
  instance, you might first want to reach out to your allies who share your
  vision and who you have a trusted relationship with, both to get their
  support and feedback. Then, you might turn to the opponents, with
  whom you share a trusted relationship, to get critical feedback before
  moving on to the low-trust stakeholders.

Agreement

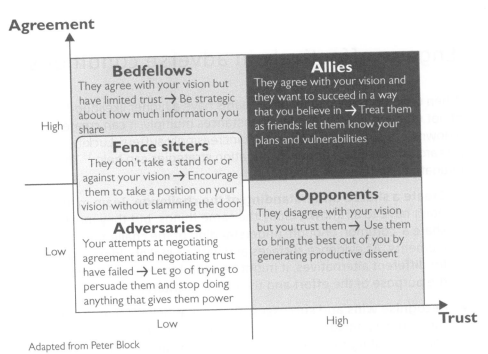

Bedfellows
They agree with your vision but have limited trust → Be strategic about how much information you share

Allies
They agree with your vision and they want to succeed in a way that you believe in → Treat them as friends: let them know your plans and vulnerabilities

Fence sitters
They don't take a stand for or against your vision → Encourage them to take a position on your vision without slamming the door

Opponents
They disagree with your vision but you trust them → Use them to bring the best out of you by generating productive dissent

Adversaries
Your attempts at negotiating agreement and negotiating trust have failed → Let go of trying to persuade them and stop doing anything that gives them power

High | Low

Low | High | **Trust**

Adapted from Peter Block

- **Leverage consistency.** Get stakeholders to commit to your recommendations actively, publicly and voluntarily. People want to be and appear consistent across actions, statements, and beliefs. So, if we can get people to commit their support early, it's a lot easier to actually secure it down the line. Concretely, you should have one-on-one conversations with key stakeholders ahead of submitting your recommendations to them as a group.

- **Create scarcity or a shrinking window.** Whether we recognise it or not, we tend to find opportunities that are in short supply more desirable than plentiful ones.[11] That propensity to avoid scarcity closely relates to our built-in preference to avoid losses, which manifests itself with us preferring to take a sure thing over a gamble, even when the gamble has a higher expected payoff.[12] So what? Well, in practical terms, you may want to formulate your recommendations so that stakeholders feel that following them would help them avert losses.

Engage effectively in adverse conditions

When conditions are challenging, teams have a higher likelihood of not meeting objectives. If such instances multiply, it can create a downward spiral where teamwork increasingly suffers. Luckily, research shows that adopting mitigation strategies can help.[13] These mitigation strategies include:

- **Create a shared understanding of the challenge.** Team members don't have to all know exactly the same things, but they must share a 'common enough' understanding of the challenge's key elements. As evidence surfaces and various stakeholders advocate for different alternatives, it might be useful to remind everyone of the purpose of the effort and the decision criteria.

- **Recognise wins and successes.** Teams that believe that they can succeed despite adverse conditions are known to perform better. Communicating the team's successes – large and small – can be an effective way to do so. So if the team is in an impasse, it might be worth reminding the team that it has overcome other impasses before or that disagreement has led to better outcomes.

- **Build psychological safety.** Recall from previous chapters that psychological safety is the extent to which people on the team feel that they can admit mistakes, voice a dissenting opinion, or acknowledge confusion without risking being rejected or penalised. A strong predictor of team effectiveness, psychological safety is particularly important when the team leader cannot see everything and must instead rely on the team to speak up and ask questions.[14]

- **Actively boost team resiliency.** Team resiliency is the team's capacity to withstand and bounce back from adversity. Highly resilient teams minimise the impact of stressors by anticipating challenges from the outset and by conveying to their team that the journey will have many ups and downs, and that this is to be expected. Doing so helps team members create a growth mindset in the team. The adoption of a *growth mindset* (the belief that intelligence and talent can be improved) has been shown to help people work through setbacks in a more constructive manner than when they adopted a fixed mindset (the belief that talent and intelligence are static).[15] In addition, leaders can help by assessing emerging challenges, adroitly guiding the team between 'normal' and 'emergency' modes, and providing timely updates.

MEET THEM WHERE //// THEY ARE AND SHOW THEM //// WHERE YOU'RE GOING

Don't wait for your presentation to your stakeholders to find out that some are opposed to your ideas. Instead, time permitting, engage them individually to gauge their level of support (or opposition) and better understand what resonates with them.

A question we often hear at this stage is, should you tell your audience where you're going first or should you let them get to their own conclusions? Well, let's find out. Read the following paragraph.

> A newspaper is better than a magazine. A seashore is a better place than the street. At first it is better to run than to walk. You may have to try several times. It takes some skill but it's easy to learn. Even young children can enjoy it. Once successful, complications are minimal. Birds seldom get too close. Rain, however, soaks in very fast. Too many people doing the same thing can also cause problems. One needs lots of room. If there are no complications, it can be very peaceful. A rock will serve as an anchor. If things break loose from it, however, you will not get a second chance.

You're probably intrigued. What if we told you first that what we're thinking of is making and flying a kite; would you read it differently?[16]

The point is that if you don't tell your audience upfront where you are going, they will only be able to follow you for a bit before getting lost in the details. Then, once they understand your overall point, they need to revisit all previous points to check whether they agree. If, on the other hand, you tell them where you are going first, they can more effectively integrate new information as it comes.

On the other hand, suspense and tension can be powerful tools to create engagement with your audience.[17] For instance, raising a question at the beginning of your presentation and getting your listeners to think about why it matters, and what potential answers might be, can create a strong hook, building interest and curiosity for what comes later.

Dedicating all your efforts on the analysis to just wing the engagement part is not the best use of your limited resources. However, there is no one right way to set up your communication. It depends on factors such as the type of presentation, the audience, and your timeframe. The key point is to engage deliberately, which requires you thinking through these questions before reaching out to your stakeholders.

Too much of a good thing? The case for limiting engagement

Throughout the book, we make the case that engaging stakeholders is beneficial. But there is such a thing as too much engagement: One of us was recently helping a multinational that has allowed its will to engage stakeholders extensively significantly slow down its decision making. It's not just a decision speed issue, engaging also has a cost for all parties that might end up being higher than the value of engagement. If the people engaged are only peripherally related to the decision, you might create a sense of waste and increase opportunity costs.[18] Your challenge then is to create optimal engagement, where you include people who can add value and you ask them to contribute where their input is the most useful. To do so, it might be useful to:

- **Clarify responsibilities.** Decision makers need to hold the appropriate *responsibility* (the ownership of making the decision), *authority* (the ownership of the power and resources needed to make the decision), and *accountability* (the ownership of the credit or blame for the decision process and its outcome). Along the decision process, the responsibility often passes from one group to another; when that happens, the authority and accountability must also shift.[19]

- **Clarify the rules of engagement.** Not all people in the decision team need to have the same influence. Some might just be consulted; others might have a vote; others still might have a veto power. It is important to create an accurate and shared mental model of the team roles and responsibilities.[20]

PART MATRICES, PART PYRAMIDS – CREATE A ROBUST MESSAGE

Preparing to deliver your recommendations to an audience – be it a one-to-one conversation or with a larger group – it is useful to clarify what you want that conversation to achieve. A from/to matrix can help you do so: it lays out in one column what your audience currently thinks (or does) and in another column what you want them to think (or do) as a result of your communication.[21]

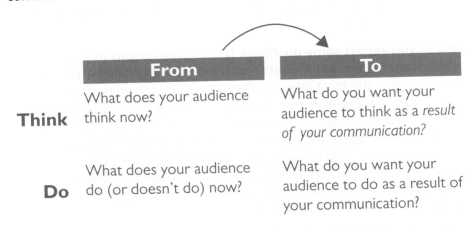

	From	**To**
Think	What does your audience think now?	What do you want your audience to think as a *result of your communication?*
Do	What does your audience do (or doesn't do) now?	What do you want your audience to do as a result of your communication?

Depending on your problem and audience, you are likely to encounter differing levels of support. Some might be highly supportive from the outset, and all you need to do is lay out the plan of action to get the implementation started. Others might be more critical of what you are about to propose and will require to be convinced more deliberately.

Although it is always challenging to find an appropriate angle for these different situations, FrED gives you concrete avenues, depending on how much pushback is expected.

Expect significant pushback? Start by summarising what's important—the criteria —then proceed to 2

Expect little pushback? Describe your preferred alternative

		Affordability	Speed	Comfort	Greenness	Score	Rank
	Weight:	0.1	0.3	0.5	0.1		
	By taking a plane	50	75	100	40	82	1
How should I go from NYC to London?	By taking a helicopter	25	50	75	25	58	3
	By taking a balloon	25	0	50	75	34	4
	By taking a rocket	0	100	0	0	27	5
	By taking a boat	100	25	100	0	73	2

Expect some pushback? Start by explaining which alternatives you discarded (and why), then proceed to step 1

- **When you expect little pushback (1)**, you can directly present your chosen alternative and explain why the decision was made. This approach can be conveyed quickly as it only focuses on the alternative that was selected.

- **When you expect some pushback (2)**, jumping directly to your chosen alternative might create resistance. You might be better off first outlining the most relevant alternatives you considered and their trade-offs, starting with those that you ended up discarding. Only then explain why you chose your alternative. Although some people may continue to disagree, this approach underscores that you considered various avenues. That conveys procedural fairness (see Chapter 6), which increases the likelihood that critics, although potentially still disagreeing with the outcome, will at least understand and respect why you made that decision in that way.

- **If you expect *significant* pushback (3)**, go back to the basics. You may start with covering what's important to the stakeholders – that is, the treasure and the decision criteria. Doing so will also help you sensitise the audience that different people care about different things and that the tensions among these different objectives can't be easily reconciled.

For instance, you might point to the tensions between ensuring short-term success *and* long-term survival or the tensions between the objectives of your shareholders who are focused on financial returns *and* those of your internal stakeholders, like the union members, who are prioritising job security and working conditions. Next, you might review the available alternatives, starting with those that you ended up discarding. Go over each alternative's trade-offs as doing so will make your thinking more transparent. Finally, present the alternative that you ended up selecting. Don't just present its positives, also cover where it falls short and explain why, overall, you feel that the alternative still has a better overall profile than the others. It will still be a challenging moment, no doubt, but you are more likely to be able to show that you have taken the different perspectives into consideration than if you directly present your chosen alternative.

No matter which approach you choose, the broader point is that you should try to meet your audience where they are before taking them to where you want them to be.

MECE thinking matters for engagement

Presenting your findings to your stakeholders, you will need to skilfully structure your message. Here, too, pushing for MECEness can help avoid creating confusion and making people nervous.

Imagine that you're recommending to improve your company's profitability by reducing fixed costs and, in addition, shutting down a factory. People might ask: 'Wait, is closing a factory part of the efforts to reduce fixed costs, or is it something else?' The source of confusion here is that the two proposed measures partially overlap.

Furthermore, recommending to improve your company's profitability by reducing fixed costs without mentioning other avenues than shutting down the factory might leave your audience wondering if you even considered alternatives. In other words, if you're not collectively exhaustive, your audience gets nervous and wonders whether they can trust you.

→

On the other hand, if you lay out early on a MECE classification of the alternatives, they are less likely to wonder whether you left out what was important to them. Think of this classification as defining 'mental buckets' (recall Chapter 4). Creating sensible mental buckets at the outset generates structure and interest, prompting your audience to continue engaging with you, instead of checking their phone after your first bullet point.

How Apple restructured its product portfolio after it had almost gone bankrupt in the mid-90s exemplifies how MECE thinking can help provide clear direction to an organisation. When Steve Jobs returned to Apple in 1997, the company had a broad product portfolio (another adjective instead of 'broad' might be 'messy') consisting of many Power PCs, notebooks, digital notepads and peripherals, including printers and cameras. Instead of developing new ideas and business models, Jobs' first action was to clean up the portfolio. As he said at the time: 'The product line up was too complicated and the company was bleeding cash. A friend of the family asked me which Apple computer she should buy. She couldn't figure out the differences among them and I couldn't give her clear guidance, either.'[22] He and his team did so by using a simple MECE structure: professional user and private user for the customer segments, and desktop and notebook for the product category, which gave Apple a simple four-quadrant matrix that defined their product portfolio going forward.

The simplicity of this categorisation provided clarity internally as designers, engineers and market-facing teams now knew what was in scope and out of scope. It also helped customers and business partners better understand Apple's products.

In short, MECE thinking is not just powerful for your analysis, it is also powerful to provide clear communication structures for your internal and external stakeholders.

Having defined what you want to communicate, you will also need to identify the level of detail that you want to get into. Here, it might be useful to organise your message as a pyramid, which helps you use an appropriate level of detail without omitting important parts. To this end, you may start with your key message – the top of your pyramid – before drilling down into details as needed. Your key message boils down to a phrase or two, which summarises what you're going to tell them: 'I'm here to recommend that we increase revenues by focusing our efforts to get clients from our main competitor to shift to us. Here's why.'

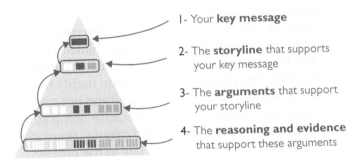

1- Your **key message**

2- The **storyline** that supports your key message

3- The **arguments** that support your storyline

4- The **reasoning and evidence** that support these arguments

Your key message relies on your storyline – the handful of ideas that work together to support your conclusion. Each of these ideas consists of arguments, each of which uses reasoning and evidence.

Organising your message in such a pyramid, you can best plan what to present given the time that's allocated to you and the level of support needed for each part.

TRANSITION FROM BEING OPEN TO BEING BULLETPROOF

It is commendable to be open-minded during the problem-solving process, but this flexibility might be misunderstood as indecisiveness, if you still display it when presenting your recommendations and explaining the way forward to the rest of the organisation. In the words of a senior executive we recently interviewed, 'when presenting to my board, I can't be seen as arrogant, but I need to have answers'. Therefore, at some point, you need to switch your mindset from problem-solving mode, where you gather feedback and insights from others to help you identify a great solution, to 'selling' mode, where you convince a broader audience of your chosen path without getting caught in detailed discussions about the quality of your solution.

Moving into selling mode requires you to change how you engage. The FrED tools, including the *why* and *how* maps, decision matrices and on-balance decisions, will help you structure your thinking processes in a way that makes them amenable to getting constructive feedback from your stakeholders. Yet, showing your decision matrix to a broader audience, who might be unfamiliar with the topic and not necessarily constructive, is often not a good idea. Why? Because doing so can open a Pandora's box of debate and dissent around criteria, alternatives and evaluations that you don't want to have this late in the process.

The picture of a cruise ship is a useful illustration of how you should be judicious about which tools you reveal to different audiences. Big cruise ships have up to 20 decks, where often only the upper decks are accessible to the passengers. Even though the cargo, kitchen, and engine decks are critical, they remain out of sight. Instead, passengers stroll around the upper decks, moving from the pool to the restaurants to the movie theatre and back to their cabin without seeing the supporting operations.

Similarly, FrED's tools are important to help you reach solid conclusions – they are the cargo, kitchen and engine decks of your analysis – but you don't necessarily want to show them to your broader stakeholders. There, you want to keep the focus on the overall storyline, perhaps supported by a few key visuals and clear recommendations. And, in case there is pushback, you want to have a sufficient grasp of your alternatives to be able to explain why you made the decision you made. But you don't want to expose all the details of your efforts.

We highlight this point because we often have participants in our programmes who enjoy working with FrED's frameworks and processes so much that they want to share them with their broader audience. Often, however, this does not end well as their audience divert the flow of the presentation to focus on unintended aspects.

One final note about getting into selling mode: It's not because you're trying to convince others that you need to provide false certainty. Although it is widely accepted that people prefer to receive advice that appears certain, recent research finds that this hypothesis might need to be revisited.[23] In short, instead of pretending that you know for sure what will happen, you might acknowledge whatever inherent uncertainty there is: 'based on what we see today, we are 70% confident that the best option is X, but we also acknowledge that there is inherent uncertainty, and therefore we'll continue monitoring the situation frequently to change course swiftly if needs be.' We'll continue our discussion of uncertainty in the next chapter.

///////// CHAPTER 8 TAKEAWAYS /////////

Even the greatest analysis isn't enough. To convert your strategy into a solution, you need to synthesise your findings into a compelling argument that will convince your stakeholders.

Don't make your final reveal one big surprise! Instead, and time permitting, win stakeholders one at a time ahead.

Appealing to logic might only take you so far. Sometimes, skilfully appealing to emotions or character (the three legs of the Aristotelean persuasion stool) might be more effective. In the end, your message should blend them.

Creating a powerful storyline doesn't have to be an obscure art. As with the rest of FrED, structuring your effort can guide you: identify what you want to achieve (from/to matrix), meet your audience where they are (at the criteria for high pushback; at the discarded alternatives for medium pushback; at the preferred alternative for little pushback), and build your message (pyramid).

Transition from being open during the problem-solving process to being bulletproof when presenting recommendations and explaining the way forward.

///////// CHAPTER 8 NOTES /////////

1 See, for instance, Bartunek, J. M. (2007). 'Academic-practitioner collaboration need not require joint or relevant research: Toward a relational scholarship of integration.' *Academy of Management Journal* **50**(6): 1323–1333. Stucki, I. and F. Sager (2018). 'Aristotelian framing: Logos, ethos, pathos and the use of evidence in policy frames.' *Policy Sciences* **51**(3): 373–385.

2 Is ethos really working? Some rhetoricians argue that appealing to ethos has the most important impact over the long run (Bartunek, J. M.

(2007). 'Academic-practitioner collaboration need not require joint or relevant re search: Toward a relational scholarship of integration.' *Academy of Management Journal* **50**(6): 1323–1333.). But some research has found the effect of credibility to be underwhelming (Hample, D. and J. M. Hample (2014). 'Persuasion about health risks: evidence, credibility, scientific flourishes, and risk perceptions.' *Argumentation and Advocacy* **51**(1): 17–29.).

3 See p. xviii of Rosenzweig, P. (2007). *The halo effect ... and the eight other business delusions that deceive managers*, Free Press.

4 Yet again, pathos > logos. Unfortunately. For an example of a balanced, logic argument losing against an emotional-but-anecdotal one, see Moore, D. A. (2021). 'Perfectly confident leadership.' *California Management Review* **63**(3): 58–69.

5 See p. xi of Haidt, J. (2006). *The happiness hypothesis: Finding modern truth in ancient wisdom*, Basic Books.

6 I'm going with *this* guy. For an example of how you can start with evaluating alternatives before coming to a conclusion, see Colin Powell's endorsement of Barack Obama during the 2008 US presidential race. In the video, Powell, a lifelong Republican, doesn't start with his conclusion. Instead, he devotes the first six minutes to evaluating the qualities of Obama and McCain using clear criteria. Only then does he conclude that Obama is the more promising candidate. (Glaister, D. (2008). Colin Powell endorses Barack Obama for president. *The Guardian*) Video available at: https://www.youtube.com/watch?v=b2U63fXBlFo.

7 Seo, M.-G. and L. F. Barrett (2007). 'Being emotional during decision making—good or bad? An empirical investigation.' *Academy of Management Journal* **50**(4): 923–940. For a review of usefulness of emotions, see Bartunek, J. M. Ibid. 'Academic-practitioner collaboration need not require joint or relevant research: Toward a relational scholarship of integration.' (6): 1323–1333.

8 Arthur, C. (2011). Nokia's chief executive to staff: 'we are standing on a burning platform. *The Guardian*.

9 See Cialdini, R. B. (2001). 'The science of persuasion.' *Scientific American* **284**(2): 76–81. Cialdini, R. B. and N. J. Goldstein (2002). 'The science and practice of persuasion.' *Cornell Hotel and Restaurant Administration Quarterly* **43**(2): 40–50.

10 See pp. 128–149 of Block, P. (2017). *The empowered manager: Positive political skills at work*. Hoboken, New Jersey, John Wiley & Sons.

11 Lynn, M. (1991). 'Scarcity effects on value: A quantitative review of the commodity theory literature.' *Psychology & Marketing* **8**(1): 43–57.

12 On loss aversion, see, for instance, pp. 731–732 of Adler, R. S. (2005). 'Flawed Thinking: Addressing Decision Biases in Negotiation.' *Ohio St. J. on Disp. Resol.* **20**: 683, Arceneaux, K. (2012). 'Cognitive biases and the strength of political arguments.' *American Journal of Political Science* **56**(2): 271–285.

13 Tannenbaum, S. I., A. M. Traylor, E. J. Thomas and E. Salas (2021). 'Managing teamwork in the face of pandemic: evidence-based tips.' *BMJ Quality & Safety* **30**(1): 59–63.

14 For an in-depth coverage of the concept of psychological safety, see Edmondson, A. (2019). *The fearless organization*, Wiley.

15 For a more in-depth discussion of the growth mindset concept, see Carol, D. (2007). *Mindset*, Ballantine Books. For supporting evidence of adopting a growth mindset, see Yeager, D. S., P. Hanselman, G. M. Walton, J. S. Murray, R. Crosnoe, C. Muller, E. Tipton, B. Schneider, C. S. Hulleman, C. P. Hinojosa, D. Paunesku, C. Romero, K. Flint, A. Roberts, R. Iachan, J. Buontempo, S. Man Yang, C. M. Carvalho, P. R. Hahn, M. Gopalan, P. Mhatre, R. Ferguson, A. L. Duckworth and C. S. Dweck (2019). 'A national experiment reveals where a growth mindset improves achievement.' *Nature* **573**(7774): 364–369.

16 Bransford, J. D. and M. K. Johnson (1972). 'Contextual prerequisites for understanding: Some investigations of comprehension and recall.' *Journal of Verbal Learning and Verbal Behavior* **11**(6): 717–726.

17 See, for instance, pp. 63–97 of Heath, C. and D. Heath (2007). *Made to stick: Why some ideas survive and others die*. New York, Random House.

18 De Smet, A., G. Jost and L. Weiss (2019). 'Three keys to faster, better decisions.' *The McKinsey Quarterly*.

19 See pp. 11–12 of French, S., J. Maule and N. Papamichail (2009). *Decision behaviour, analysis and support*, Cambridge University Press.

20 De Smet, A., G. Jost and L. Weiss (2019). 'Three keys to faster, better decisions.' *The McKinsey Quarterly.* See also Rogers, P. and M. Blenko (2006). 'Who has the D.' *Harvard Business Review* **84**(1): 52–61.

21 We've stolen the 'from/to matrix' from Andrew Abela, who calls it a 'From-to/Think-Do' matrix; see pp. 29–34 of Abela, A. (2008). *Advanced presentations by design: Creating communication that drives action*, John Wiley & Sons.

22 Steve Jobs quoted on p. 13 of Rumelt, R. P. (2011). *Good strategy/bad strategy: The difference and why it matters.*

23 Gaertig, C. and J. P. Simmons (2018). 'Do people inherently dislike uncertain advice?' *Psychological Science* **29**(4): 504–520.

Chapter Nine
—

Go!

So, having framed, explored, and decided, we have now identified our strategy. Or, have we? Hard to tell, under uncertainty. Chapter 9 shows how you can better manage uncertainty through adopting a probabilistic mindset. In addition, it shows how to further improve your problem solving by honing your skills and focusing on the process rather than the outcome. The chapter concludes showing how FrED can help you make big decisions in just a few minutes.

Let's first look at managing uncertainty. Despite our best efforts, it is likely that our conclusions still partly rely on assumptions. Not only that, but circumstances might also have changed during the problem-solving process; after all, it's not because we have finished our analysis that the environment has stopped evolving or that new evidence has stopped appearing.

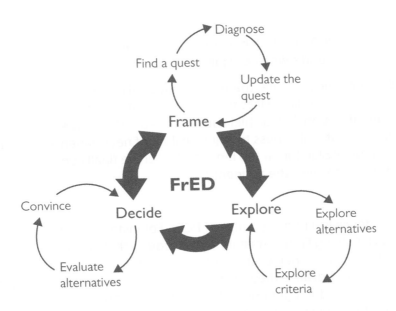

So, how should we deal with changing circumstances? Continuing with a strategy when we should change is called 'plan continuation bias' or PCE (for 'plan continuation error'); it's a prevalent bias at the origin of the Torrey Canyon oil spill and a plethora of less-visible mishaps.

The Torrey Canyon supertanker fails to update its course

In the early morning of Saturday, 18 March, 1967, the first officer of the supertanker Torrey Canyon corrected the ship's course after realising that it wasn't where it was supposed to be. The 300-metre ship was carrying 120,000 tonnes of crude oil north past the Scilly Isles, just off the coast in South West England.

When sleep-deprived captain Rugiati woke, he countermanded the first officer's change.[1] He was under a tight deadline to reach his destination at high tide, and the two-hour detour that the first officer had initiated might mean waiting for five days for a new window. So Captain Rugiati stuck to his original plan, going through the Scilly Isles instead of around them. This decision had a monumental environmental impact as the ship ran aground spilling its cargo of crude over a 300-km stretch of British and French coasts in what was at the time the world's worst oil spill.

Aside from time pressure, the Torrey Canyon also suffered from other issues, including a less than ideal navigation system and poor equipment design. Yet, a chief cause of the accident appeared to be Captain Rugiati's slowness to adjust in light of new evidence. He stuck to his original plan for far too long, and when he finally updated it, it was too late to avert the accident.[2]

Overconfidence is a primary cause of PCEs. For instance, a study of accidents involving French military aircraft found that, in a majority of cases (54%), the crew persevered not because they failed to process information but because they trusted too much their ability to manage risk. What's more, we don't get out of these conditions on our own: 80% of the recoveries from perseveration included outside intervention.[3]

The aviation community treats errors as symptoms of deeper issues,[4] and it takes systematic, evidence-based steps to reduce them. So we might be well inspired to learn from it. For instance, setting personal weather minimums under which a pilot would cancel an ongoing landing procedure is a deliberate practice.[5] What would be an equivalent mitigation approach for strategic decision making in organisations? Well, adopting a two-pillar approach might help:

- **Predetermine a rule to continue with the current strategy:** For instance, you might ask yourself, what would it take to change my mind (that, say, our chosen strategy remains the best course of action)? What early indicators of success (or lack thereof) would we expect to see within a few days, weeks or months of rolling out our strategy? Be especially clear on the data that would lead you to decrease your confidence in your conclusions or even change your mind as to how to move forward. This is the data that we don't want to see but that we need to see.

- **When conditions change, stick to that predetermined rule:** Although it might sound trivial that we ought to adhere to the rule that we developed for ourselves ahead of stressful situations, empirical evidence shows that in the heat of the moment we tend to throw caution to the wind. Some analyses of pilots, for instance, showed that nearly everyone (96.4% of test subjects) violated the rules that they had set for themselves ahead of the flight, choosing instead to adopt a more dangerous course of action.[6] To help you be one of the remaining 3.6%, remember that you can enlist the help of a commitment device, such as a Ulysses' contract (see Chapter 1).

ADOPT A PROBABILISTIC MINDSET

//// ////

Le doute n'est pas une condition agréable, mais la certitude est absurde.[7]

– Voltaire (Lettre à Frederick II de Prusse 6 avril 1767)

Having gone through a FrED cycle, evaluate your confidence that the strategy you selected is what you ought to do, from 0 (not at all confident) to 100 (absolutely sure).

Quantify your confidence (or lack thereof)

In philosopher and mathematician Bertrand Russell's words, 'Everything is vague to a degree you do not realise till you have tried to make it precise'. That observation is particularly salient for the evaluation of probability. In fact, people interpret likelihood labels (e.g. very likely, unlikely, roughly even odds) in different ways, sometimes *vastly* different ways, so you will be well served to evaluate your confidence numerically (from 0 to 100).[8]

Almost no chance	Very unlikely	Unlikely	Roughly even chance	Likely	Very likely	Almost certain(ly)
1–5%	5–20%	20–45%	45–55%	55–80%	80–95%	95–99%

Adapted from Office of the Director of National intelligence

Some detractors of this approach often point out that numerical estimates aren't particularly intuitive to most people. However, Dartmouth's professor of government Jeff Friedman offers a different take: 'Most people are between the ages of 0 and 100. When you see a stranger, you can usually narrow down a plausible range for that person's age. Maybe, all else being equal, you think that person is between 30 and 50 years old. If you have no other information, you take the midpoint, 40. Maybe that seems a bit low, so you increase your estimate to 42. I believe that few people would find that logic to be complex or unusual.

All probabilities are between 0 and 100%. When you're asked to estimate the chances that a statement is true, you can usually narrow down a plausible range for what that probability should entail. Maybe, all else being equal, you think that probability is between 30 and 50%. If you have no other information, you take the midpoint, 40%. Maybe that seems a bit low, so you increase your estimate to 42%. From a logical standpoint, it's really no different than estimating a stranger's age.

So why do we intuitively think that estimating probabilities is odd? I think the answer is that we don't have much opportunity to calibrate our judgments about uncertainty.

Over the course of your life, you get lots of feedback about what 42-year-old people look like. If I ask you to think about a 42-year-old person, you can probably conjure up a concrete image of what that entails. By contrast, uncertainty is abstract and very few people spend the time and effort to calibrate their assessments of uncertainty. Thus, it's no surprise that people find it hard to consider what a 42% chance 'looks like'. But that isn't grounds for thinking that probabilistic reasoning is invalid or inappropriate: it's just a reason to spend more time and effort figuring out how to reason in rigorous ways.[9]

Watch out for overconfidence

When we ask executives to rate their confidence in the conclusions of an analysis they just conducted, many report being highly confident (often at 80% or higher).

But note that your confidence in your conclusions depends on your confidence in your quest, alternatives, criteria, and evaluations – and those are multiplicative, so any weakness in your analysis transfers to your conclusions!

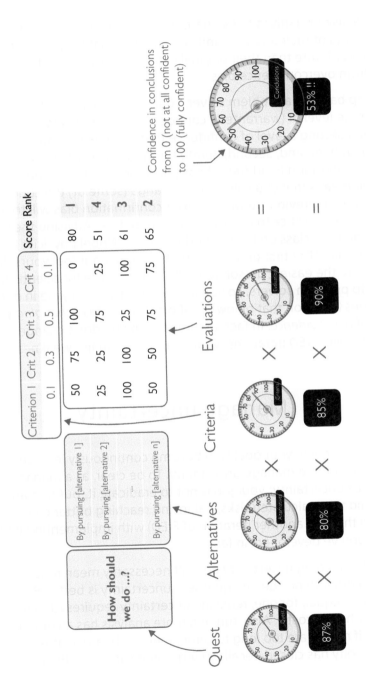

Confidence in conclusions from 0 (not at all confident) to 100 (fully confident)

	Criterion 1	Crit 2	Crit 3	Crit 4	Score	Rank
	0.1	0.3	0.5	0.1		
	50	75	100	0	80	1
	25	25	75	25	51	4
	100	100	25	100	61	3
	50	50	75	75	65	2

Evaluations

Criteria

Alternatives

| By pursuing [alternative 1] |
| By pursuing [alternative 2] |
| ... |
| By pursuing [alternative n] |

How should we do ...?

Quest

90% × 85% × 80% × 87% = 53% !!

When we ask executives to evaluate their confidence in each of the four components of their analysis, and we highlight that they multiply to a much lower figure than their original estimate, they realise that they might suffer from overconfidence bias.

If we step back, as a problem solver, your objective should be to reach an appropriate level of (warranted!) confidence in your results. That you can do by first setting a level of confidence that you feel is appropriate for the problem at hand and, second, iterate through consecutive FrED cycles, using each iteration to address the weakest point(s) in your analysis. Watch out! That means that you will need to change (some of) the conclusions you reached in previous iterations. Your confirmation bias will try its best to make you stick to what you thought before. Advising the Caltech 1974 graduating class on being good scientists, Nobel physicist Richard Feynman said, 'The first principle is that you must not fool yourself – and you are the easiest person to fool'.[10] What is true for scientists also applies to problem solvers, so you'll have to actively engage in debiasing techniques (more on that below). In short, *take pride in changing your mind in light of new evidence*. In fact, assume that if you don't change your mind drastically over FrED iterations, your analysis has major weaknesses.

Manage uncertainty

With this approach, your goal is to become continuously less wrong, which means you need to manage uncertainty. To be clear, as a manager, you *always* face uncertainty; your job is not to eradicate it, but to manage it.[11] You should take calculated risks, balancing reaching better conclusions (by going through another iteration of FrED) with implementing whatever strategy you've developed so far.

Note that managing uncertainty doesn't necessarily mean reducing it. Of course, all other things being equal, less uncertainty is better. But all other things aren't equal; for one, reducing uncertainty requires running more analysis, which is costly. Also, running more analysis has an opportunity cost, and if results are too long to come, they might arrive after your window of opportunity has closed (recall Boeing's predicament in the prologue).

So, you shouldn't aim at being sure that you've found the 'right' answer, but at being reasonably confident that you've found a fantastic/excellent/good-enough answer.[12] Recognising that a good-enough answer executed swiftly often beats a brilliant one implemented slowly, you might decide that, for some of your problems, you're better served shooting for 60% confidence in your strategy rather than a 90%.[13]

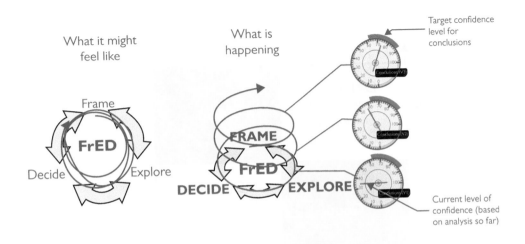

Adopting such a probabilistic mindset requires embracing failures. If you move ahead with less than a 100% confidence in your results – as you should – expect that you *will* be wrong at times. And that's okay. Think of your decisions as a portfolio. Some will be excellent, others will be acceptable, others still won't be glorious. But, as a whole, your portfolio will be all right.

A corollary is that you'll have failures to learn from. Yes, failures are painful, but they provide a fertile ground for learning, possibly more fertile than successes.[14] Mastery takes failing. Nobody sat down in front of a piano for the first time and played Schubert's Forelle flawlessly. In that sense, failing isn't the opposite of succeeding, but an integral part of succeeding. What matters is to keep the price of failing manageable, taking appropriate risks.[15] That's achievable in two ways: reducing the probability of failures and reducing their impact.

Reduce the probability of failures

If you're overconfident, you'll take risks that you don't suspect, making failures more probable. Similarly, if you're overconfident, you might spend too much time strategising at the expense of executing, which can also result in failures. So, reducing the probability of failures requires that you calibrate your confidence level to your abilities.[16]

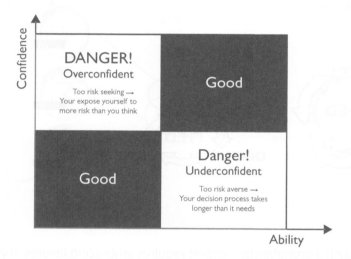

One way to reduce overconfidence is to not trust our intuition but, rather, *test* our intuition, continuously aiming to prove it wrong. To do that, ask yourself 'what evidence would change my mind?' and then seek that opposing evidence. In the end, your preferred answers shouldn't be the ones that have the most supporting evidence, but those that best withstand the strongest critical-thinking attacks.

A good way to do so might be to develop what psychologist Adam Grant calls a challenge network, a group of people you trust to point out your blind spots.[17]

Reduce the impact of failures when they occur

No matter how hard we try to prevent them, failures *will* occur. So, we can't just rely on avoiding them, we must also be good at correcting them. Indeed, there is growing recognition that error prevention must be complemented with error management: approaches to effectively deal with errors after they have occurred.[18]

Try this! Create effective debriefs

Debriefs (or 'after-action reviews') are used in the medical community, the aviation industry, the US army and countless other settings to promote experiential learning through systematising reflection, discussion, and goal setting. Research has shown that they can improve individual and team effectiveness significantly.[19] So it might be beneficial to set up effective debriefs.

From a 2013 meta-analysis, psychologists Tannenbaum and Cerasoli observed that aligning participants, intent, and measurement yields the greatest effects, but even 'misaligned' debriefs demonstrate reasonable efficacy.[20]

Debriefs are a wonderful opportunity to praise good teamwork and point out improvement opportunities. When debriefing a negative event, it is important to emphasise *what* went wrong not *who* was wrong and how the team can prevent it from happening in the future.[21]

Having a documented FrED process handy will help you understand where you could have avoided mistakes. Just by looking at the matrix you can review whether you focused on a poor quest, missed worthy alternatives, omitted relevant criteria, evaluated the alternatives poorly, or misread trade-offs. In short, a well-documented FrED enables you to be more granular in your after-action review. Conversely, if all you have to look back to is a description of the one idea that you recommended and why it is great, it is frequently impossible to retrace the decision process to understand where things went sideways.

Gaining this FrED-powered, in-depth understanding can help you identify whether suboptimal results originated from mistakes or bad luck. Based on this insight, you can work on your systems and processes to mitigate the avoidable mistakes going forward; say, by investing more in exploring alternatives, being more thoughtful with your decision criteria, or working through the trade-offs more deliberately.

////// UPDATE YOUR THINKING //////

So far, all we have to show for our problem-solving efforts is a hypothesis of what we think might be a good solution (our strategy). We ought to test that hypothesis, updating our thinking as new evidence surfaces. In line with the scientific thinking that has guided us throughout this book, our strategy should be a hypothesis that we continuously update. And, in case you're wondering whether that's worth all the trouble, research has shown that entrepreneurs who are trained to think like scientists have better outcomes; so, yes![22]

Adopt a Bayesian worldview

In probability theory, Bayesian thinking consists of updating one's thinking in light of new evidence. We probably lost half of you at 'probability' in the previous phrase but, if you're still reading, fear not, dear reader, as no equations are coming. The good news is you can derive some benefits of Bayesian thinking by just adopting it as a mindset.

Applied epistemologist Tim van Gelder makes a compelling case for shifting our problem-solving approach from a Boolean worldview (where everything is deterministic: either true or false; right or wrong) to a Bayesian one (everything is more or less probable from 0 (impossible) to 100 (certain)).[23]

Adopting a Bayesian worldview is useful throughout FrED. For instance, we started with a question that we thought would be a great quest. But diagnosing it brought in new evidence that led us to reframe it. Similarly, we thought of only one answer for our quest, but developing a *how* map brought in new evidence that resulted in wider solution space. Updating also helped us identify better criteria and improve our evaluations.

In fact, we should continue with constantly updating our thinking even after we reached a conclusion: As we implement our strategy, we might get new evidence showing a gap between what we predicted would happen and what actually happened. This should trigger revisiting how to proceed: maybe you'll change strategy, maybe you won't. But if you stay with the current one, that will be the result of a conscious decision, not inertia.

Improve your crystal ball

If you knew what the future looks like, you would make consistently better decisions. So, as a decision maker, you must make predictions. But as the Danish proverb goes, 'it's difficult to make predictions, especially about the future'.

Ideally, you are well calibrated, able to make a good initial guess on even an unfamiliar subject *and* updating your thinking appropriately in light of new evidence. But if you can only have one of these traits, we would argue that it is better to have the latter. An ability to recognise when you're off and course correct appropriately – that is, in so many words – is invaluable.

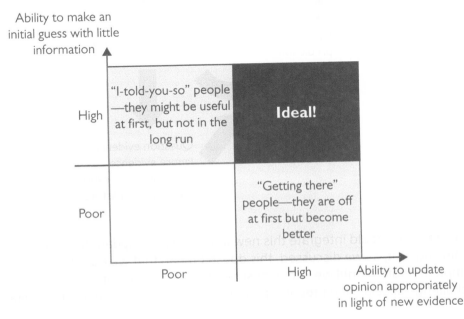

Our initial guess – called our *prior* – can throw us off in two ways. If we have too strong a prior, we will need massive amounts of opposing evidence to change our mind. This can happen to the best of us: Einstein was so set on the universe being static that he needed to add a parameter – the cosmological constant – in the theory of general relativity.[24] Conversely, too weak a prior means we need massive supporting evidence to accept it. This evidence might not be available, thereby hindering progress, as it has with various scientific advances.[25]

For many of us, observing evidence that differs from what we expect is a point where we question evidence, we ignore it, we double down on our original path, or we obfuscate and distract (not you, of course, dear reader, but think of a politician, whichever one). A quote often attributed to Winston Churchill goes, 'Men occasionally stumble over the truth, but most of them pick themselves up and hurry off as if nothing had happened.'

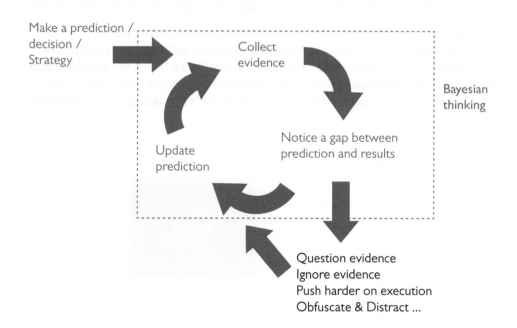

Make a prediction /
decision /
Strategy

Collect
evidence

Bayesian
thinking

Notice a gap between
prediction and results

Update
prediction

Question evidence
Ignore evidence
Push harder on execution
Obfuscate & Distract ...

Instead, we should integrate this new information to update our original thinking. But, as we discussed, this doesn't mean that we ought to delay implementation until we know for sure what's going to happen. The challenge is balancing preparing for an uncertain future with getting things done. By thinking of our strategy as a hypothesis, one that we continuously update in light of new evidence, we reduce the gap between strategy and execution as we see these elements as interdependent activities that will benefit from greater integration.[26]

There are many practical implications of adopting a Bayesian worldview. Perhaps most important: If you have low confidence in some components of your decision (quest, alternatives, criteria, or evaluations), build contingency plans in your implementation so that you can course correct swiftly as you go.

Front load your implementation efforts with two-way-door decisions

One way to categorise decisions is to separate them as one-way-door and two-way-door decisions. One-way-door decisions, once made, are difficult or impossible to modify. Once you walk through that door, it shuts closed behind you and there's no handle to let you back in. Think of selling your company, quitting your job, squeezing the toothpaste out of the tube, jumping off that plane (with a parachute, of course!). Once you've jumped off the plane, it's not entirely trivial to get back into the plane.

Irreversible decision?

In 1929, the Indiana Bell Telephone Company bought an eight-story building so that they could destroy it and build a larger headquarter in its stead. But architect Kurt Vonnegut Sr (yes, the father of the novelist) suggested an alternative: move the building to make room for expansion.

Over the course of a month, using a concrete mat and hydraulic jacks and rollers, the 11,000-tonne building was shifted 16 metres south and rotated 90 degrees. Even what appears as the ultimate irreversible decision – choosing where to place a building – wasn't so definitive in the end: with some effort, even that decision could be changed.[27]

But many of our decisions are 'two-way doors'. With a little effort, they can be changed or reversed.[28] If you structure your implementation effort by front-loading it with two-way-door decisions, you retain flexibility in your plan when the uncertainty is the highest – and, therefore, your need to pivot quickly is the greatest.

Equally useful is to turn seemingly one-way door decisions into two-way doors. Consider how Richard Branson started his airline: 'When we launched Virgin Atlantic I made a deal with Boeing that we could hand the plane back in a year's time if the airline didn't get off the ground. Thankfully, we never had to. But if things hadn't worked out, I could have walked back through the door.' Branson also reduced the risks by leasing a second-hand 747 rather than a new one.[29]

///////////// HONE THE SKILLS /////////////

Like improving any higher-order skill, improving your ability to solve complex problems requires deliberately investing into the process while leveraging timely, constructive feedback.

Train

Research shows that training can effectively improve problem-solving skills, and, ultimately, team performance,[30] so you might want to consciously invest in improving your skills. Even if you aren't in a position to develop an organisation-wide programme, you can still progress. For instance, you might want to test how much you suffer from, say, overconfidence.[31] ClearerThinking.org provides some tools to help you self-assess.[32] Based on these insights, you can make corrections, such as changing how much you rely on your instinct.

The role of effective feedback to support learning has been extensively established.[33] So, you may want to experiment with FrED in a low-risk environment to generate such feedback. Just as pilots and surgeons use simulators to hone their skills in environments where mistakes bear no consequences, find low-stake projects that you could use as your simulators. In fact, you may use those to also develop your own checklists of what you need to pay attention to when the pressure increases.[34]

Build problem-solving habits

The tools in this book will become particularly helpful if you manage to turn them into thinking habits. Instead of pulling out the book to consult the respective chapters, once you use FrED on a few challenges, the core ideas will become second nature to you.

Think back to when you learned how to ride a bicycle. For most of us that required patience and persistence, and the occasional beat-up knee. Be similarly persistent with FrED. Your journey to better problem solving starts with realising that there are ways to approach complex problems differently than you've approached them. That doesn't mean yet that you

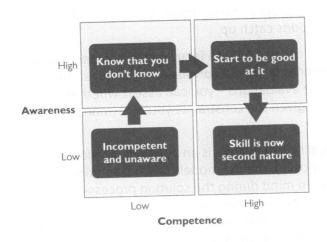

know how to follow these ways, just like having a bicycle doesn't mean that you know how to ride it. Once you've created that awareness, it pays off to consciously use the tools until you firmly grasp them, just like you practised riding your bicycle for a while before it became natural. At some point, it will become second nature.

But beware, if you stop being attentive before you have actually ingrained the new habit, you are likely to go back to the old way of doing things. This happens with some students who thoroughly enjoy using FrED while they are in class but, once they return home, they revert to their old intuitive ways.

///// FOCUS ON THE PROCESS, /////
NOT THE OUTCOME

The success of our problem-solving efforts doesn't just depend on what we put into it; luck also plays a role, which is why judging a problem-solving approach by its outcome isn't advisable.[35] After all, even a broken clock is right twice a day; we all get lucky every now and then, even when we follow a poor process. So we might get away with a poor process, but eventually the odds catch up.

Practically, you can use FrED to focus on the process. Keeping in sight the four components of your conclusion – the quest, the alternatives, the criteria, and the evaluations – you can assess whether your process is robust enough given the constraints you face (more on that in the next section).

Another critical skill to acquire is an ability to develop multiple, and potentially opposing, mental models of what solutions could look like.[36] Keeping an open mind during the solution process enables you to evolve these models – keeping what's useful and eliminating what is not – before you come to a conclusion. Author F. Scott Fitzgerald pointed to the importance of this skill when he wrote, 'The test of a first-rate intelligence is the ability to hold two opposing ideas in mind at the same time and still retain the ability to function.'[37]

Although sticking to a deliberate process is important to manage time and mental space, be mindful to not overengineer your process. We sometimes see executives invest disproportionate effort and ultimately fail to develop a solution because they run out of time.

HOW TO SOLVE COMPLEX PROBLEMS IN FIVE MINUTES

//// ////

FrED can be a good guide if you have weeks or months to solve your problem, but every now and then, you walk into a meeting room to discover that you must make a high-stake decision on the spot. What should you do if you only have a few minutes to think through a complex problem?

Well, FrED's usefulness remains, as you can use it to mentally check the validity of your thinking. Under time pressure you won't have the ability to go deep into any of the steps, but you can still run through all of them at a high level by asking yourself:

- Are we focusing on a good **quest**? (frame)
- Are we considering enough **alternatives**? (explore)
- Are we using an appropriate set of evaluation **criteria**? (explore)
- Are we using good-enough **evaluations**? (decide)

These questions also come in handy any time you find yourself in a heated debate about the best way forward. Instead of digging your heels in your preferred alternative ('I failed to convince them so far but, surely, if I shout!?'), asking yourself these questions will help you understand your interlocutor's goals, how she thinks about the alternatives, and what she is willing to trade off – three key insights to have *before* getting into a debate about what's the best way forward.

Of course, if all that fails, there's always shouting.

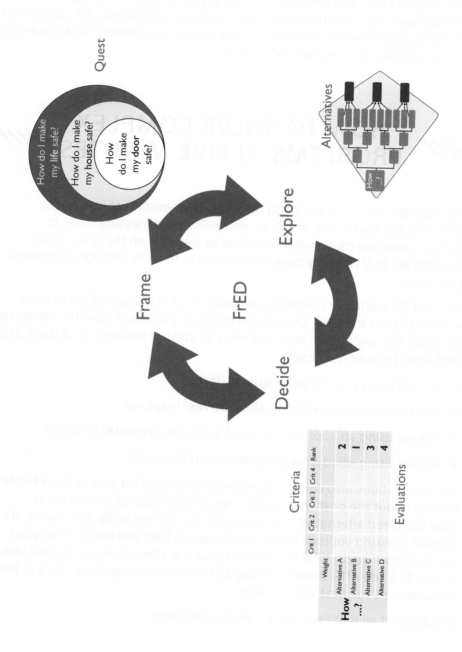

//////// CHAPTER TAKEAWAYS ////////

The quality of your analysis depends on the quality of the quest, alternatives, criteria, and evaluations. These aren't compensatory, so you need a minimum level for each.

Calibrate your confidence on the quality of your analysis: don't be too confident simply because you've run an analysis.

Rather than trusting your intuition, *test* it. Be evidence-based, looking primarily for opposing evidence.

Chances are you are wrong about a lot of what you think. Nothing personal, we all are! Identify what you can do about it. In short, be open-minded. Given your specific constraints, try to find a good balance between learning more (being less wrong) and moving forward.

Use FrED iteratively, focusing each cycle on the weakest part of your analysis and adopting a Bayesian approach: update your thinking in light of new evidence. Don't hesitate to change your mind if the evidence warrants it!

Even when there is no time to use the tools fully, following FrED can help you think in a more structured way; use it as a roadmap.

//////// CHAPTER 9 NOTES ////////

1   Espresso, anyone? Although sleep deprivation damages your decision-making abilities, it appears that caffeine mitigates these negative effects. See Killgore, W. D., G. H. Kamimori and T. J. Balkin (2011). 'Caffeine protects against increased risk-taking propensity during severe sleep deprivation.' *Journal of Sleep Research* **20**(3): 395–403.

2   It's not just *beauty* sleep. In the Torrey Canyon accident, notice how Captain Rugiati was sleep deprived, which might have contributed to his unwillingness to adjust his thinking. Experiments have shown that sleep deprivation can result, among many other things, in irrational risk

taking. See Barnes, C. M. and N. F. Watson (2019). 'Why healthy sleep is good for business.' *Sleep Medicine Reviews* **47**: 112–118. See Chauvin, C. (2011). 'Human factors and maritime safety.' *The Journal of Navigation* **64**(4): 625. Harford, T. (2019). Brexit lessons from the wreck of the Torrey Canyon. *Financial Times*. Rothblum, A. M. (2000). *Human error and marine safety*. National Safety Council Congress and Expo, Orlando, FL.

3   Bourgeon, L., C. Valot, A. Vacher and C. Navarro (2011). *Study of perseveration behaviors in military aeronautical accidents and incidents: Analysis of plan continuation errors*. Proceedings of the Human Factors and Ergonomics Society annual meeting, SAGE Publications Sage CA: Los Angeles, CA.

4   For references, see p. 764 of Miranda, A. T. (2018). 'Understanding human error in naval aviation mishaps.' *Human Factors* **60**(6): 763–777.

5   Winter, S. R., S. Rice, J. Capps, J. Trombley, M. N. Milner, E. C. Anania, N. W. Walters and B. S. Baugh (2020). 'An analysis of a pilot's adherence to their personal weather minimums.' *Safety Science* **123**: 104576.

6   Winter, S. R., S. Rice, J. Capps, J. Trombley, M. N. Milner, E. C. Anania, N. W. Walters and B. S. Baugh (2020). 'An analysis of a pilot's adherence to their personal weather minimums.' *Safety Science* **123**: 104576.

7   Uncertainty is an uncomfortable position, but certainty is an absurd one.

8   See, for instance, Office of the Director of National Intelligence (2015). Analytic standards. Intelligence community directive 203. Dhami, M. K. and D. R. Mandel (2021). 'Words or numbers? Communicating probability in intelligence analysis.' *American Psychologist* **76**(3): 549. Beyth-Marom, R. (1982). 'How probable is probable? A numerical translation of verbal probability expressions.' *Journal of Forecasting* **1**(3): 257–269. Wintle, B. C., H. Fraser, B. C. Wills, A. E. Nicholson and F. Fidler (2019). 'Verbal probabilities: Very likely to be somewhat more confusing than numbers.' *PloS One* **14**(4): e0213522. Also, see pp. 25–26 of National Research Council (2006). *Completing the forecast: Characterizing and communicating uncertainty for better decisions using weather and climate forecasts*, National Academies Press, Office of the Director of National Intelligence (2015). Analytic standards. Intelligence community directive 203. See also pp. 84–85 of National Research Council (2011). *Intelligence*

analysis: behavioral and social scientific foundations. Washington, DC, National Academies Press.

9 Friedman, J. (2020). 'Analytic rigour is improved by probabilistic thinking and communication.'

10 Feynman, R. P. (1974). 'Cargo Cult Science.' *Engineering and Science* **37**(7): 10–13.

11 Another take on your job as a manager. We contend that your job, as a manager, isn't to eradicate uncertainty but to manage it. Management scholar Roger Martin phrases it slightly differently: 'the objective is not to eliminate risk but to increase the odds of success' (Martin 2014).

12 This relates to the idea of a *requisite decision model*: a model is considered requisite when it provides enough guidance to decide upon a course of action. Phillips, L. D. (1984). 'A theory of requisite decision models.' *Acta Psychologica* **56**(1-3): 29–48. See also pp. 55–56 of Goodwin, P. and G. Wright (2014). *Decision analysis for management judgment*, John Wiley & Sons.

13 For practical ways to avoid bottlenecks in organisational decision making, see Rogers, P. and M. Blenko (2006). 'Who has the D.' *Harvard Business Review* **84**(1): 52–61.

14 Failing is an integral part of succeeding. For a discussion of how to frame failure in a positive way, see pp. 160–164 of Milkman, K. (2021). *How to change: The science of getting from where you are to where you want to be.* London, Vermilion.

15 For practical suggestions on how organisations can re-balance their risk portfolios, see Lovallo, D., T. Koller, R. Uhlaner and D. Kahneman (2020). 'Your company is too risk averse: Here's why and what to do about it.' *Harvard Business Review* **98**(2): 104–111.

16 For more on confidence calibration, see Moore, D. A. (2021). 'Perfectly confident leadership.' *California Management Review* **63**(3): 58–69.

17 See Chapter 4 of Grant, A. (2021). *Think again: The power of knowing what you don't know.* New York, Viking.

18 See Frese, M. and N. Keith (2015). 'Action errors, error management, and learning in organizations.' *Annual Review of Psychology* **66**: 661–687.

19 Tannenbaum, S. I. and C. P. Cerasoli (2013). 'Do team and individual debriefs enhance performance? A meta-analysis.' *Human Factors: The Journal of the Human Factors and Ergonomics Society* **55**(1): 231–245.

20 Ibid.

21 See p. 65 of Tullo, F. J. (2010). Teamwork and organizational factors. *Crew resource management*, Second edition. Barbara Kanki, Robert Helmreich and J. Anca. London, Elsevier: 59–78.

22 Camuffo, A., A. Cordova, A. Gambardella and C. Spina (2020). 'A scientific approach to entrepreneurial decision making: Evidence from a randomized control trial.' *Management Science* **66**(2): 564–586.

23 van Gelder, T. (2014). Do you hold a Bayesian or a Boolean worldview? *The Age*. Melbourne.

24 Nussbaumer, H. (2014). 'Einstein's conversion from his static to an expanding universe.' *The European Physical Journal H* **39**(1): 37–62.

25 Bang, D. and C. D. Frith (2017). 'Making better decisions in groups.' *Royal Society Open Science* **4**(8): 170193.

26 Edmondson, A. and P. Verdin (2017). 'Your strategy should be a hypothesis you constantly adjust.' *Harvard Business Review*.

27 Aldrich, S. (2010). Kurt Vonnegut's Indianapolis. *National Geographic*.

28 Gregersen, H. (2021). 'When a leader like Bezos steps down, can innovation keep up?' *Sloan Management Review*.

29 The Telegraph (2018). Sir Richard Branson: The business of risk. From https://www.youtube.com/watch?v=-49524mB49520gY.

30 McEwan, D., G. R. Ruissen, M. A. Eys, B. D. Zumbo and M. R. Beauchamp (2017). 'The effectiveness of teamwork training on teamwork behaviors and team performance: A systematic review and meta-analysis of controlled interventions.' *PloS One* **12**(1): e0169604.

31 Incompetent and unaware. People tend to overestimate their abilities in many social and intellectual domains. See Kruger, J. and D. Dunning (1999). 'Unskilled and unaware of it: How difficulties in recognizing one's own incompetence lead to inflated self-assessments.' *Journal of Personality and Social Psychology* **77**(6): 1121.

32 Clearer Thinking. (2021). 'Make better decisions.' Retrieved 30 July, 2021, from https://www.clearerthinking.org.

33 See, for instance, pp. 52–53 of National Research Council (2011). *Intelligence analysis for tomorrow: Advances from the behavioral and social sciences*. Washington, DC, National Academies Press.

34 For an example of the usefulness of checklists, see Gawande, A. (2007). *The checklist*. For an in-depth discussion, see Gawande, A. (2009). *The checklist manifesto*. New York, Picador.

35 Don't judge by the outcome. Evaluating a decision by its outcome rather than its process is called outcome bias or 'resulting'. For more, see Baron, J. and J. C. Hershey (1988). 'Outcome bias in decision evaluation.' *Journal of Personality and Social Psychology* **54**(4): 569; and pp. 1–24 of Duke, A. (2020). *How to decide: Simple tools for making better choices*, Penguin.

36 For a detailed, hands-on approach on the usefulness of mental models, see Martin, R. L. (2009). *The opposable mind: How successful leaders win through integrative thinking*, Harvard Business Press.

37 Fitzgerald, F. S. (1936). The crack-up. *Esquire.*

RECOMMENDATIONS FOR FURTHER READING

Algorithms to live by (Christian and Griffiths 2016) shows how applying some guiding principles of computer science can help with making professional and personal decisions.

Think again (Grant 2021) offers practical ideas from the social sciences to help keep an open mind when dealing with uncertainty.

Decisive (Heath and Heath 2013) summarises advances in social sciences into an insightful framework to sidestep psychological traps while making difficult decisions.

Give yourself a nudge (Keeney 2020) gives concrete ways to improve your decision making, focusing particularly on the criteria.

Perfectly confident (Moore 2020) provides practical ideas to test hypotheses and think probabilistically.

Range (Epstein 2020) argues that breadth can be valuable and provides compelling support that what's obvious isn't necessarily desirable.

Superforecasting (Tetlock and Gardner 2015) uses empirical findings to identify concrete actions that help people deal with uncertainty.

What's your problem? (Wedell-Wedellsborg 2020) contributes a deep dive into the framing step with many practical and engaging ideas to frame better.

ADDITIONAL REFERENCES

National Research Council (2015). *Measuring human capabilities: An agenda for basic research on the assessment of individual and group performance potential for military accession*. Washington, DC, National Academies Press.

Scopelliti, I., et al. (2015). 'Bias blind spot: Structure, measurement, and consequences.' *Management Science* **61**(10): 2468–2486.

Ehrlinger, J., et al. (2016). 'Understanding overconfidence: Theories of intelligence, preferential attention, and distorted self-assessment.' *Journal of Experimental Social Psychology* **63**: 94–100.

FEEDBACK

We are interested in hearing from you. We appreciate both supportive and critical feedback, which can help us improve our future research work. Please get in touch with us at arnaud.enders@imd.org and albrecht.enders@imd.org.

Lausanne, March 2022

ABOUT THE AUTHORS

Arnaud Chevallier is Professor of Strategy at IMD. Arnaud's research, teaching and consulting on strategic thinking synthesise empirical findings from diverse disciplines into concrete tools to improve decision-making and problem solving. His previous book, *Strategic Thinking in Complex Problem Solving*, provides a deep dive into epistemic considerations in problem solving.

At IMD, Arnaud is the director of the Global Management Foundations programme, which is a core component of the executive MBA, and the master's of science in Sustainable Management and Technology offered jointly with EPFL and Unil. He also directs various custom programmes.

He has worked in diverse industries with numerous organisations, including Cisco; Gavi, the Vaccine Alliance; the International Committee of the Red Cross; Novo Nordisk; Shell; SAP; Statkraft; the United Nations and Tetra Pak.

Prior to IMD, Arnaud was an associate vice provost at Rice University and the graduate dean of the University of Monterrey before that. Earlier, he worked in Accenture's strategy and business architecture practice out of Houston and London.

A French and US citizen, Arnaud has worked in Mexico, the United States, the United Kingdom and Switzerland. He holds a BS and ME in mechanical engineering from the Université de Versailles and an MS and a PhD in mechanical engineering from Rice University.

Albrecht Enders is Professor of Strategy and Innovation at IMD. His major research, teaching and consulting interests are in the areas of managing discontinuous change and top team strategy development processes. He is also the co-director of IMD's Transition-To-Business Leadership Program (TBL). Before coming to IMD, Albrecht worked as a consultant with The Boston Consulting Group.

Albrecht's research has appeared in leading academic journals such as *Administrative Science Quarterly, Academy of Management Journal,*

Academy of Management Review and *Research Policy*, and practitioner-oriented outlets including *Harvard Business Review*, *MIT Sloan Management Review* and *The Financial Times*. His research and case writing efforts have been recognised by awards from the BPS division of the Academy of Management, the EFMD, ECCH and SIM.

Albrecht holds a PhD in strategic management from the Leipzig Graduate School of Management in Germany and a BA in economics from Dartmouth College in the United States.

AUTHORS' ACKNOWLEDGEMENTS

—

Our names are on the cover, but this book came to life only with the help of many wonderful people. We are deeply indebted to our executive students, advisors, co-authors, colleagues and the many other people who contributed to, hopefully, making us a little less wrong.

For the production of this book, we are particularly indebted to Friederike Hawighorst whose stellar fact-checking left us no respite! Not only did she painstakingly challenge each of our assertions, but she did so in an inspiring way. Thank you for your wonderful contribution, Friederike; we can't wait to hear about your upcoming successes—and we'll be the first to tell people that we knew you way back when!

IMD is a unique sandbox. At the intersection of the world of ideas (academia) and that of doing (management), it enables us to generate ideas, develop them and relentlessly test them in empirical settings. That makes our job unbelievably fun. Any more fun, in fact, and we'd feel compelled to forgo our salary.

IMD's unique DNA stems from diverse, fun, brilliant people working together—plus us two, who aspire to be half as talented as them. We are indebted to our many colleagues here. Among them, we send particular appreciation to Jean-Louis Barsoux, Cyril Bouquet, Christos Cabolis, Dominik Chahabadi, Antoine Chocque, Frédéric Dalsace, Lisa Duke, Delia Fischer, Susan Goldsworthy, Lars Haggstrom, Paul Hunter, Tawfik Jelassi, Amit Joshi, Blandine Malhet, Jean-François Manzoni, Alyson Meister, Anand Narasimhan, Kiyan Nouchirvani, Francis Pfluger, Patrick Reinmöller, Karl Schmedders, Dominique Turpin and Michael Watkins. Phil Rosenzweig gets special thanks for directly (Albrecht) and indirectly (Arnaud) bringing us to IMD, serving as a role model of rigour and pedagogy during our tenure here, providing deeply insightful comments on an early version of the draft, and generally challenging us to be better thinkers and educators.

Participants in our programmes significantly contributed to shaping the material. We are especially grateful to those in the MBA, Executive MBA, Advanced Strategic Management, Advanced Management Concepts, Global Management Foundations, Transition to Business Leadership, Orchestrating Winning Performance and Complex Problem-Solving programmes.

We also benefited immensely from the help of numerous individuals in academia and the business world who through the space of an email exchange, joint teaching, a dinner conversation, a walk along the lake, or a review of the draft offered wonderful ideas. We extend special gratitude to Max Bazerman, Jeff Friedman, Marc Gruber, Dirk Hoke, Jouko Karvinen, Philip Meissner, Gilles Morel, Fred Oswald, Martin Reeves, Denise Rousseau, Richard Rumelt, Ian Charles Stewart, Phil Tetlock, Tim van Gelder and Thomas Wedell-Wedellsborg and Torsten Wulf.

Others yet helped us improve how we approach complex problems in ways big and small. We're grateful to TJ Farnworth, Øystein Fjeldstad, Harald Hungenberg, Thomas Hutzschenreuter, Ajay Kohli, Michael Kokkolaras, Andreas König, François Modave, Paula Sanders, Pol Spanos, Siri Terjesen, Petros Tratskas and Michael Widowitz for sharing insightful ways into cracking tough problems.

We also thank the staff at Pearson Education and in the IMD Communication team for bringing this project to life.

Finally, we are most grateful to our extended families—in Germany, France, and the US—for their love, advice, patience, humour and support through-out the journey. They continuously put up with us when FrED kept us away from family activities over countless evenings, weekends and vacations. Now that FrED is out in the world, we only hope to show them as much support as they have. Our lives are better because you're in them; thank you!

PUBLISHER'S ACKNOWLEDGEMENTS

PHOTO CREDITS:

56 Alamy Images: Shawshots/Alamy Stock **Photo; 30 Anne-Raphaelle Centonze:** Courtesy of Anne-Raphaelle (de Barmon) Centonze. Used with Permission.

TEXT CREDITS:

3 PwC Global: Adapted from PWC (2017). The talent challenge: Harnessing the power of human skills in the machine age; **8 American Psychological Association**: Kahneman, D., & Klein, G. (2009). Conditions for intuitive expertise: A failure to disagree. American Psychologist, 64(6), 515–526; **8 John Wiley & Sons, Inc.**: Evans, D. (2003), Hierarchy of evidence: a framework for ranking evidence evaluating healthcare interventions. Journal of Clinical Nursing, 12: 77-84. https://doi.org/10.1046/j.1365-2702.2003.00662.x; **8 The National Academies Press**: National Research Council. 2011. Successful K-12 STEM Education: Identifying Effective Approaches in Science, Technology, Engineering, and Mathematics; **10 John Maynard Keynes:** This quote is attributed to John Maynard Keynes with some controversy, as there are also sources that list economist Paul Samuelson as having coined a similar phrase; **27 The Irish Times:** Adapted from Irish Times (1997). Pope's fancy footwork may have saved the life of Galileo; **32-33 National Library of France:** Bibliothèque nationale de France. (2015). "Le château de Versailles, 1661–1710 – Les fontainiers." Retrieved 11 May 2021, from http://passerelles.bnf.fr/techniques/versailles_01_6.php; **34 Juan Manuel Fangio:** Quoted by Juan Manuel

Fangio; **37 Harvard Business Publishing:** McKee, R. and B. Fryer (2003). "Storytelling that moves people." Harvard Business Review 81(6): 51-55; **46 Elsevier:** Ginnett, R. C. (2010). Crews as groups: Their formation and their leadership. In Crew resource management (pp. 73-102). Academic Press; **48 Academy of Management:** Nutt, P. C. (1999). "Surprising but true: Half the decisions in organizations fail." Academy of Management Perspectives 13(4): 75-90; **54 George E. P. Box:** Quoted by George Edward Pelham Box; **57-58 Richard Post Rumelt:** Quoted by Richard Post Rumelt; **58 Anton Chekhov:** Quoted by Anton Chekhov; **59 Anton Chekhov:** Quoted by Anton Chekhov; **62-63 Michael Merkel:** Quoted by Michael Merkel; **66 Flannery O'Connor:** Quoted by Novelist Flannery O'Connor; **64 The National Archives:** Air Accidents Investigations Branch (1990). Report on the accident to Boeing 737-400 G-OBME near Kegworth, Leicestershire on 8 January 1989 (Aircraft Accident Report 4/90). HMSO. London; **83 Jouko Karvinen:** Quoted by Jouko Karvinen; **84 Juan Carlos Bueno:** Quoted by Juan Carlos Bueno; **103 Alex Osborn:** Quoted by Alex Osborn; **103 Linus Pauling:** Quoted by Linus Pauling; **103-104 Thomas Alva Edison:** Quoted by Thomas Alva Edison; **115 Roger L. Martin:** Martin, R. (1997). Strategic choice structuring – A set of good choices positions a firm for competitive advantage; **132 Sage Publications:** Hofstede, G. (2001). Culture's consequences: Comparing values, behaviors, institutions, and organizations across nations, Sage Publications; **146 Richard Post Rumelt:** Quoted by Richard Rumelt; **149 JørgenVig Knudstorp:** Quoted by JørgenVig Knudstorp; **149 Roger Martin:** Quoted by Roger Martin; **150 Henri Poincaré:** Quoted by Henri Poincaré; **158 Stanford Graduate School of Business:** Burgelman, R. A., M. Sutherland and M. H. Fischer (2019). BoKlok's Housing for the Many People: On-the-Money Homes for Pinpointed Buyers. Stanford Case SM298A; **159 Michael Porter:** Quoted by Michael Porter; **164 Abraham Maslow:** Quoted by Abraham Maslow; **171-172 Guardian News & Media Limited:** Arthur, C. (2011). Nokia's chief executive to staff: 'we are standing on a burning platform. The Guardian; **173 Peter Block:** Adapted from Peter Block; **175 Christopher West:** Quoted by Christopher West; **180 Steve Jobs:** Steve Jobs quoted on p. 13 of Rumelt, R. P. (2011). Good strategy / bad strategy: The difference and why it matters; **191 Snieders, F:** Voltaire (Lettre à Frederick II de Prusse 6 avril 1767); **191 Bertrand Russell:** Quoted by Bertrand Russell; **191 Office of the Director of National Intelligence:** Adapted from Office of the director of National Intelligence; **192 Jeffrey Friedman:** Friedman, J. (2020). "Analytic rigour is improved by probabilistic thinking and communication";

194 Richard P. Feynman: Feynman, R. P. (1974). "Cargo Cult Science."
Engineering and Science 37(7): 10–13; **200 Winston Churchill:** Quoted
by Winston Churchill; **201 National Geographic:** Aldrich, S. (2010). Kurt
Vonnegut's Indianapolis. National Geographic; **202 The Telegraph:** The
Telegraph (2018). Sir Richard Branson – The business of risk: https://www.
youtube.com/watch?v=-49524mB49520gY; **204 Hearst Magazine Media,
Inc.:** Fitzgerald, F. S. (1936). The Crack-Up. Esquire

INDEX

Page numbers followed by 'n' refer to notes.